# jubilat

## twenty one

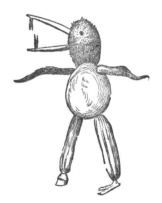

FOUNDER
Robert N. Casper

PUBLISHER
Emily Pettit

EDITORS
Kevin González
Caryl Pagel

MANAGING EDITOR
Anne Holmes

EDITORS-AT-LARGE
Jen Bervin
Christian Hawkey
Terrance Hayes
Cathy Park Hong
Evie Shockley
Michael Teig

ASSISTANT EDITOR
Gale Thompson

ASSISTANT MANAGING EDITOR
Kristen Evans

WEB EDITOR
Heather Christle

DESIGN EDITOR
Guy Pettit

CONTRIBUTING EDITORS
Andrew Beccone
Jedediah Berry
Jessica Fjeld
Peter Gizzi
Kimiko Hahn
Matthea Harvey
Eric Keenaghan
Andrew Kenower
Brett Fletcher Lauer
Jeffrey Lependorf
Lisa Olstein

ISSN: 1529-0999

EDITORIAL ASSISTANTS
Lizzie Lenson
Ted Powers
Mike Wall

READERS
Sarah Boyer
Stella Corso
Ben Roylance

jubilat is published twice yearly at the
University of Massachusetts, Amherst.

*Business & Editorial Address:*
jubilat
Department of English
482 Bartlett Hall
University of Massachusetts
Amherst, MA 01003-9269

*Subscriptions:* Individuals $14 per year or
$26 for two years. Institutions $28 per
year or $52 for two years. Please add $5
for Canadian and foreign subscriptions.
Single issues are available for $8.

Distributed by Ingram and Ubiquity.

jubilat is funded in part by the
National Endowment for the Arts,
the Massachusetts Cultural Council,
& the UMass Arts Council.

For information on how to submit,
please visit us at www.jubilat.org.

© 2012 jubilat. No portions of jubilat
may be reproduced without permission.

This publisher is a proud member of

COUNCIL OF LITERARY MAGAZINES & PRESSES
www.clmp.org

NATIONAL
ENDOWMENT
FOR THE ARTS

# Contents

Cover art by Jono Tosch

# WAS PRETTY WAS KIDS

*Shane McCrae*

Was pretty was kids

said I looked / Like Michael Jackson Michael Jackson 1982

And skinny sometimes    wouldn't eat for days

Was pretty and he saw it    was / Pretty he saw it too

Pretty for boys / To be a boy

Pretty it made him angry talked as if

It made him angry talked / Why

would I want to look like that / And didn't look at me    I thought

He didn't like me knew he

didn't like niggers and I was one    was half

Niggers and I was one    and wasn't also wasn't

old enough to be    afraid of him

the way a man    / Would

without love

he held me down face down

# *from* AGONISTES

*Joshua Edwards*

## DAYS OF SHAKING OUT RUGS

I should be much for open war, O peers—
My eldest brother is an astronaut.
The truth is, I have no older brother.
In fact, I am an astronaut myself.
I am the world's only real astronaut,
I'll recede into space before your eyes!
I was born an orphan and do become
More of an orphan as I grow older.
All my years I've spent in this town, alone
But for those who made me eat my carrots.

If you have ever returned from a trip
Abroad and found your country completely
Changed, then you know how I have always felt.
I once thought it a simple problem of
Geography—that I was born ten hours
Late, that the globe had spun beneath my soul
Too much, and when I did at last descend
I animated an American
Instead of a nascent whale or some babe
Destined for wealth and greatness in Japan.

Later, once I had learned that God is dead
But there is a striving and adaptive
Spirit in all forms of life, I shifted

The blame to History—the ugliest
Story I've ever heard, and one whose gore
I can never seem to turn away from.
I was born too late or too early or
I shouldn't have ever been born at all.
Then I ended up on a sofa and
Learned about Freud and dreams I didn't have.

Although most of it seemed phony, the source
Of my constant discomfort became clear:
The world is made by men and women, made
In fits and starts when they are without love.
That was and is where I rest my case: Love
Itself is good for nothing but killing
Time, and the desire to make the future
Into a circumstance to be survived.
What remains if thou lovest nothing well?
If you said "emptiness," then you are wrong.

Emptiness itself means well when well-wrought,
But love not well-wrought is its opposite,
Which, mind you, is not hate—it is revenge.
And so, when I looked to the stars and saw
Only the darkness between them, I knew
That our world's time in the heavens should end.
I am building a machine that will bring
A comet into congress with the earth,
To return the ether to its peaceful
Anonymity, without a subject.

From my bedroom I'll hear morality
Cry out as its contradictions collapse

Upon mankind—we who used it against
One another in our arguments and wars.
The belief that death is some cave or hole
Has led us to use life as a weapon.
Only by destroying death's ladder's rungs
Can we bring eternity back to life.
We are none of us innocent; that word
Itself is evil wherever applied.

No, evil is not a strong enough word,
For evil has an end, but innocence
Is a daisy chain of hurting people.
When you hear someone laughing, is your first
Impulse not to think they're laughing at you?
Defending the indefensible is
Life—everyone knows how cruel children are.
Still, it is not cruelty that I loathe.
I do not loathe, I only love, as well
As any other imperfect lover.

But love itself is breaking, as a boy's
Voice breaks under maturity's burdens—
A girl captures his imagination
With her smile, his bicycle seems too small,
And his baseball cards turn into paper.
Once upended, the world is never free.
Still, my love is strong for all waves and groups
Of people, and for them I raise a glass
And toast a way to end our suffering,
A way to end it all without murder.

If your refrigerator crushed you would
You call it a killer with your last breath?
No, you would cry and think of sandwiches.
Such is my plan to bring relief to us.
Heaven will fall upon the earth, and we
Will be subsumed into our universe.
I have read hundreds of religious texts,
Seven thousand books of philosophy,
And a million pamphlets of poetry.
None of them contains an ounce of wisdom.

They are merely tired lists of arguments,
Digressions on beginnings and endings,
Rules for abattoirs and birthday parties.
The question that we really want answered
Is what will happen to our precious souls?
Such a question can only be answered
With a sincere apology, and now
Only the sky's violence is sincere.
I see this end in our future, and now
Be the prophet and the fulfiller one.

## Black Conjunction Days

Wrap yourself in a cloak of autumn, see
Evergreens and fog around you, look down
At a trail of blood on the forest floor.
Follow it to a crying child, hands pressed
To forehead, trying to hold pain at bay.
Thenceforth he grew up fearful and forlorn—
Hero of a nasty bildungsroman,
Victim of the forces of conception.
That youth was mine twenty years ago and
My voice is the voice of that little boy.

I was thirteen in 1991.
I had just arrived at the orphanage
From the streets, where at least I'd known my place
And the secret warmth of the ungoverned.
On the outside I had been cared for by
People who lived in a state of merely,
And they guarded me in my blamelessness,
But when I arrived at that place designed
To protect me, I joined a crowd whose minds
Hunted purity and exalted spoil.

Their leader, a giant boy named Art whose
Teeth were the color of a yellow dog,
Hated the way I spoke—the lively words
I found in books offended his dull ear.
I tried to explain to him how my life
Had mostly been spent in libraries and
Beneath overpasses, that my mind was
A native of the lands in classic tales.
Biography evoked no sympathy,

In fact, it probably made my plight worse.

They called me Time Traveler, Chickenshit,
Englishman, and a dozen other names.
Following Art's lead, the children pushed
Me around and made up cruel stories
About the parents I had never had.
As history may be made by rumor
And imagination dwells most on loss,
I assembled my legend from their lies
And from stories I had read: my father
Was a count and my mother his mistress.

Despite my books, I had no idea that,
While I was getting punched in the stomach,
Children only a few miles away were
Waiting with antique toys on Persian rugs
For postmen to bring them puzzles from France.
Had I known, I would have broken street lamps
And gnashed my teeth at all soft things' shadows.
My tormenters were me plus the knowledge
That our lot in life was shit, and I'm sure
In their place, I'd have beat the new boy too.

A ghost is vacancy and weakness wrapped
Around an outlook of uncertainty.
The poor are born as ghosts, invisible
As yeomen from a distant tower,
Unseen until they approach the castle
With torches lit and anger in their eyes.
How much blood has been shed for the pleasure
Of an embroidered towel or the crude

Comfort of an ottoman by a hearth.
At the thought of such things I clench my jaw.

On top of badgering by cruel boys
I suffered the joyless nuns' attention
And lived in fear of their dark afterlives,
Fearing also blood, wine, flesh, and demons
That could enter my heart if I misspoke.
To sin is to lie to the emperor
Upon whose silver platter the future
Will be served, is what my keepers taught me.
I made of my resentment a great wall
To hold back the sea of their bad ideas.

It would seem by this account that my time
Among Hell's children and the wives of God
Was brief, but it lasted several dull
And cruel (yet unmemorable) years,
Until I managed to escape one night
Into the freedom of my prior life
Of discarded food and ambient warmth.
Trains thundered over the quivering bridge
Under which I slept many moonless nights.
The city's stench commingled with my own.

I thought of moving to the countryside,
Where solitude is sweetened by birdsongs
And scenes are unspoiled by the eyes of men.
Another time I thought to build an ark
And await the flood I was sure to come.
And another I considered moving
Into a cave to contemplate the truth

Until I emerged with all the answers.
Then one day I came into possession
Of a timeworn German dictionary.

In German there is a word for spirit
That also means mind, and that's the meaning
I chose, since choosing meant to be something—
I thought until I learned German letters.
Turns out, to be something is to choose it.
The value is in being, not in choice,
And if the value of being is low,
There can be no other choice than to raze
The foundations of all future prisons.
I myself could change the world's direction.

# Agrarian

*Natalie Lyalin*

In a photograph I kiss a horse and look foreign

Blood makes me faint but I still go for it

A goat dies

Something changes in my eyes and I am terrifying

A light comes on or goes off

Blindly, I hoof it around the barn kicking at things

That pig diseased me, I think

A darkness comes and goes without settling

Today the moon was a black circle in a mud sky

Tomorrow the sun will blind me

In a fugue state I lick my fur parts clean and roost

Hello, I am a new type of animal

There are gaggles of us out in the country

We are singing within our mother tongues

Our mother's tongues, we are using them

Sometimes I say my name is Kelly from Ohio

Sometimes I am more mythical

I am a great angry thing with thick feathers

I am hiding rings in my rose-stank mouth

# A Lemon Sweat Over Everything

You can find my bones in the sister mountains

Identify me by the gold fangs

The fangs I showed you in the lemon orchard

Almost two hundred years ago

You said they were sexy

The sun blinding you from my mouth

We were both smirking

And then I snarled

It was very foreign

Chasing you around the trees

# God From the Eighth Floor

*Tomaž Šalamun*

In your lips is the life of the one
who gave life to me too.
You're borrowed, traveler!
In your eyes are waterfalls which I drink
and your hair has a fragrance of a good animal.
Don't cry, I won't snatch away.
I'm not I.
Don't shoot, you won't shoot yourself.
Do what I opened you for,
for why you're kneeling.
Pray in flesh.
You're a spring
and the white butterflies that flitter
above your naked dark skin—
wait! do you hear sirens, do you think
there's a hold up at the YMCA—
will become Tarzan
and Tarzan a big red tree.
I gave you milk, man!
Don't forget!

# FOR DAVID

It's evening.
The birds perch on the trees with a racket
and I think:
if I were my son,
would I too leaf through Larousse
before I started to talk?
Would it harm him?
Would he be amazed at this noise?
Would he ride a horse in the Sierras, young?
Tremble in front of the godlike shapes?
A green T-shirt,
a violet sweater,
the arc made by the incision between a pane
and a tin ledge—looked through a glass
of a fearsome craftsman, Maya—
on my patio?
Would Robert also visit him,
drink beer, tell how he
planted trees in the land
where it rains constantly and the Pacific
waves strike against rocks?
Does the soul extend with flesh?
Didn't the centaur keep his legs stretched out?
For if our scent leaves us,
how would the gods track us down,
they too are brittle fragile beings
like little ducks and our ancestors.


*Translated from the Slovenian by Michael Thomas Taren and the author.*

# Sorry David, David I Am So Sorry

*Francesca Chabrier & Emily Hunt*

slug in a s

now

storm

saying peace

be with you
upside down nonetheless

an indian samba

song

very well capable

of saying sorry david

david i am so sorry

about the harmonica

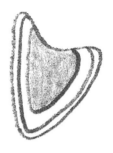

the lung like a lily......

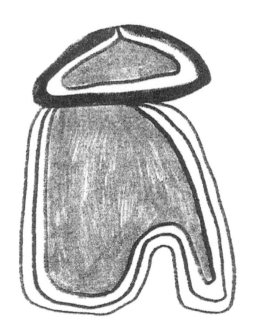

blooms on the head of another mother
watch out
for the tail end
of the road some people
be playin dominos
:: ;. :. :: :: .:

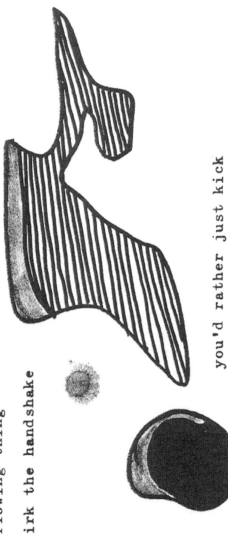

be a women in the bank a real
flowing thing

irk the handshake

you'd rather just kick

instructions for leaving for a long weekend
''upstate''

remember the aloe vera plant
is not a real child

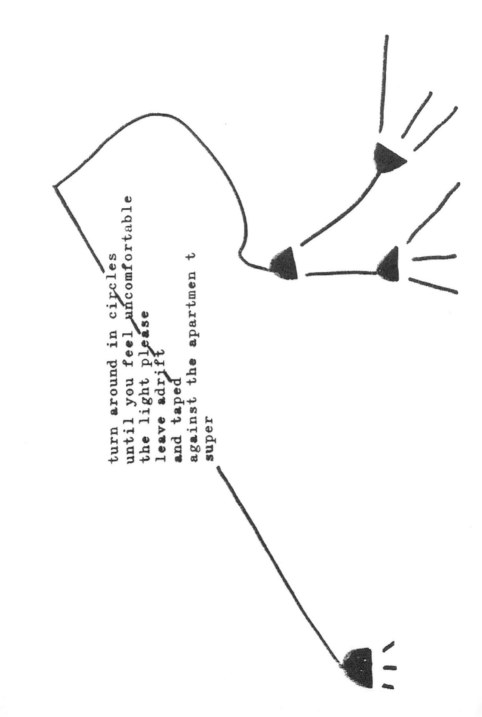

turn around in circles
until you feel uncomfortable
the light please
leave adrift
and taped
against the apartmen t
super

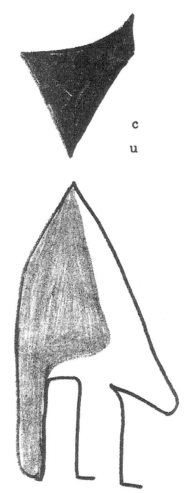

c

u

little baby 2 step

$ $ $ $ $ $ $ $ $

belly dancing

eay tour
eat your breakfast ch
child !!!!!!

moving right along...

pistol head

you're &ðôû
about

to crack
ift the line and fold
into an imaginary
pantsuit

a part of music
maintenance is being patient
the bug takes a bite
and then worms
its way

# BELLS II

*John Ashbery*

For just as a misunderstanding germinates
in a clear sky, climbing like a comma
from rack to misunderstood rack of worried clouds,
now difficult, now brusque, foregrounded, amoral,
the last birds took off into the abyss.
Now it was just us, though shielded,
separate, disparate. It almost seems—
and yet it doesn't. Broken glass announces
more offenses, home invasions. Seems like
we've been here a long time. And still
ought to do those things. Every murk is a key.

No, it's all right, don't worry.
The long-fingered peninsulas have other fish to fry
as destiny germinates on summer sands, more lap top
than lap dog. And if I'd bargain you around the aisles,
don't touch it, it's a single thing.
We don't know what breviaries are mixing cocktails for us
in the V room. It's essential we be kept
out of the cordon. You should know. This is all about you:
how you arrived one cold day carrying your little knapsack
and crept in with us, to see how we could spell.
Others than old uncles hear us now,
hacking the website's early spoilage distribution plan.

# ELECTIVE INFINITIES

Thirsty? They race across ampersands,
scrolling. He isn't sure it's his head.
There's a delay right now. Smoke backed up.
Ladies please remove hats.

It was all over by morning. The village idiot
was surprised to see us. ". . . thought you were in Normandy."
Like all pendulums we were surprised,
then slightly miffed at what seemed to be happening
back in the bushes. Keep your ornaments,
if that's what they are. Return to sender, arse.

At the intersection a statue of a policeman
was directing traffic. It seemed like a vacation,
halloween or something. Process
was the only real thing that happened.
We wove closer to the abyss, a maze of sunflowers.
The dauphin said to take our time.

# WHY IS A MOUSE SAD?

*Dorothea Lasky*

Why are mice so sad, with their crying faces

And why do they perform a shard of sadness in me

To see them

To create a mood of their scurrying

I don't know I don't know

I feel safe without them

With them, it is all horrible

Like anything could happen


Did you know that the universe

Unfolds a million times below and beneath

The scale that we exist in?

More than a million

This knowledge is astounding

It makes me realize

Just how dumb I am

And how silly we are to be afraid


Here are mice on our scale

And the universe below and beneath

And above

And airplanes

And places that scale the sky

Are just animals within the animals

And being a human is nothing

It is a construct we have created


Disregarding constructs, I want to murder all mice

I want to murder them and snuff out their sadness

And I want to flip their bodies in the air

And prevent them from enduring

An eternal sadness of being laid out

As human corpses

And the eternal sadness

Of body becoming word


What word might I transfer to a mouse

To let them know how I feel

Nothing. What words can I say to the nanoscale

To make it hear me? Nothing. It will be silence

What words can I say to the dark macrocosm

That is circling above me? Nothing.

I am dizzy. I am dizzy in its magnitude

My body is so small, it might as well not even exist, at all


In face of it all, I speak softly

In face of everything I write loud words

I color the pages of the book

Which is actually the wall

I get frightened by the shudder of the bodies next to me

Who are ghosts

Who I love despite the fact

I will never understand them


Nor will they ever understand me

Bright lights circling in some other macrocosm

Loved ones, who are ghosts, loved ones

My loved ones swirling above me

And I am so alone

And I am alone here

With the idea of ghosts

And the idea of humanity, which is a cruel idea


Humanity is a cruel idea but not a sad one

Animal ideas are sad, but only because they

Are the same as me, and I can't ever admit it

And to have a soft patch of eye and bone

Is a kind of sadness you will never get over

And to have a voice is to not have it one day, too

Which is awful

Which is much worse than to never have a body again


I think instead of being sad

At death

I'll sleep with mice

And have them crawl on my legs and hands

And I will open my eyes for them to put their eyes upon

And I will open my mouth

So that they can crawl in

And make their nest


What flattening it would be to be a mouse home

To take in the sadness

And thus negate it

And to cancel out humanity

By them inside of me

And I wouldn't let anyone kill them

If they resided within me

Not even me. I wouldn't even let myself kill them


And you

I wouldn't let you take them

With your cruel sadness

And I would no longer feel the pressure to be human

And to change my mouse behavior

And to change my behavior

Which is gentle

Which only wants to love and live

And never go away

# THE SOLDIER AND THE LION

*Nick Lantz*

*The desert. A soldier sits on a rock. A lion sits close at hand. The soldier breaks down his rifle. Laying each piece before the lion. Who gobbles it up. Then the rifle is gone.*

LION: More.

> *The soldier takes off his armor. The lion eats it.*

LION: More.

> *The soldier looks around. Finds nothing.*
> *He takes off his clothes. He is naked. The lion eats his clothes.*

LION: More.

> *The soldier stands.*

SOLDIER: What else?

> *The lion shrugs.*

LION: I don't know. But more.

SOLDIER: Couldn't I just . . .

> *He goes to leave.*

LION: No. More.

> *The soldier sits on the rock and weeps. Slowly, he takes off his foot. Gives it to the lion. Who swallows it whole.*

LION: Keep going.

> *Still weeping, the soldier takes apart his legs. And feeds them to the lion. He takes off his genitals and gives them to the lion. His ears and his nose. First the fingers of his left hand and then the whole arm.*

SOLDIER: Enough?

LION: No, more.

SOLDIER: I was sitting in my car in Ann Arbor, at a red light. It was raining. It had been raining for days. All the gutters were flooded. I had been stopped at the light for a long time. The light had turned green twice. A policeman was standing in the intersection, stopping traffic. I was angry. I wanted to get home. I wanted the streetlight to fall on the policeman. All that rain seemed worth it because it was getting the policeman so wet. I couldn't see any other cars on the street. I didn't know why he was stopping traffic. Then from behind a building came an elephant. A man was leading it by a chain. The elephant was walking down the middle of the street. Being led somewhere. I don't know where. I could hear the blood in my temples. I could feel the elephant's footsteps. I could smell it. Musty and alive. It didn't look at me. Then it passed the intersection and I couldn't see it anymore. The policeman waited a few seconds, then waved me through.

LION: Did you ever find out why it was there?

SOLDIER: I meant to, but by the time I got home, I'd forgotten about it. Can you believe that?

> *The lion looks him up and down.*

LION: About you, yes.

> *The soldier waits a moment.*

SOLDIER: That too?

LION: Even that.

> *The soldier opens his chest like a cabinet door and reaches inside. He pulls out postcards. Utensils. A shoe. A license plate. A length of rope. A dirty magazine. Cigarette after cigarette. A handful of gleaming white beach sand. Two wedding rings. A sleeping infant. This last he holds for a moment before giving it to the lion. The lion eats. Waits. A moment passes.*

SOLDIER: Who are you?
LION: Me? I'm nobody.

> *The soldier casts about with his remaining hand.*

SOLDIER: Have you seen my wallet? There was something in there.
Something.

> *The lion rises. Stretches. Leaves. The soldier*
> *calls after it.*

SOLDIER: If you see it, will you let me know?

> *He looks around. Picks up some sand, lets it fall*
> *through his fingers. He looks around.*

## END

# Arkansas

*The stage is a small-town residential street, littered with hundreds of dead birds. A man enters with a trash picker stick and a large sack. As he speaks, he collects the birds by jabbing them with the stick and depositing them in the sack.*

MAN: I hear down in the Gulf fish are washing up on beaches. Tourists don't like it. It's too crowded now, they say; the fish take the prime spots. Seagulls covered in tar wander from blanket to blanket asking for spare change. Kids are setting their sandcastles on fire.

*He shrugs.*

Who wants to see the ocean anyway? I know a guy who hasn't left his bed in ten years. Jumped off a rock into a river, thinking it was deep, but there was another rock, just under the surface, and now he doesn't go anywhere or say anything. Every half hour, someone wipes the spit from the corner of his mouth with a little square of white gauze. That's how he keeps time, probably. Maybe the gauze will be a little different today, the person handling it a little rougher or gentler. That's enough to keep a body occupied, if you ask me. Hell, he's not complaining.

People have this problem of saying things should be some other way. I shouldn't have gotten my leg blown off in the desert somewhere. I wish the mail came before noon. Gas is too expensive.

Tell you what: Learn to drive a manual transmission. Head west. Or north, or south, I don't care. Stare at the road until whenever you look away, you see the road laid over the world like a veil of gauze, that dotted line a perforation you cut along. You're the scissors, and you cut that line. Right down the middle. And on one side you've got the things the way you think they ought to be, and on the other side you've got things the way they are. But you won't be able to tell the difference. Not ever.

## END

# Mutton

*A dark strip club—oh how dark. The low stage thrusts out. At its end, a vertical pole. And wolves. Wolves at the bar, wolves in dark suits at the heart-shaped tables. Garish music: techno, electronic drum beat like tooth on bone amplified. Too loud to think. The wolves drink. The wolves talk in underwater voices. Now and then a laugh like a puncture wound. Over crackly speakers, an announcer, his enthusiasm practiced, a barbed fishhook.*

ANNOUNCER: All right, fellas, the moment you've been waiting for. Making her debut at Mutton tonight . . . Little Avery!

> *Music changes, quieter, more of a slow thump now, someone locked in a trunk, kicking. Light the color of viscera. Little Avery, a ewe, enters. A few disinterested glances tossed her way. She holds a pair of electric shears, trailing a long extension cord. Once on stage, she dances (gyrating, rubbing up against the pole, etc.).*

ANNOUNCER: Come on! Let's see it! Don't you boys want to see it? *(etc., ad lib)*

> *After a hesitation, Avery switches on the electric shears, their hornet whine clear over the music. A few wolves glance up, then go back to their drinks. Avery begins to shave the wool off her body, small patches at a time. A lone dollar bill lands on the stage, like a disinterested housefly. Nothing more. She continues.*

ANNOUNCER: Oh yes! Fellas, ain't she a sweet young thing? *(etc., ad lib)*

> *A wolf rises, crosses, Avery watching. He passes the stage, passes her, goes to the buffet, fills up a plate with hot wings, returns to his seat.*

ANNOUNCER: Here we go, boys! This is it! *(etc., ad lib)*

> *Avery finishes shaving. Everything is gone. The shears stop whining. Someone looks up, coughs. The song turns over like a bad dream. Avery retrieves the single bill, exits.*

END

ICE CREAM - New prosperity, 158
HURRICANE - Reverses for a spell, 910
HUNTING - A lost article, 162
HAMMER - Envy of neighbor, 776

GUILT - A bet won, 555

# Thomas Merton

*Jono Tosch*

Thomas Merton is actually a sandwich.
Like any sandwich,
Thomas Merton is composed of various elements.
There is the element of love.
Love is the equivalent of shredded lettuce.
In Spanish, the word for lettuce is *lechuga*.
I have some theories about this: Thomas Merton is thistle.
I understand that I have already said
Thomas Merton is a sandwich and that
sandwiches are not the same as thistle.
How could they be? Thistle grows in ditches;
sandwiches do not grow, sandwiches are made.
Thomas Merton—did he ever make a sandwich?
But how would that follow?
Can a sandwich make another sandwich?
The mute, shredded lettuce offers up its body
and the cold men surround it with a clap.
This does not bode well for love.
No one makes whoopee inside a bun.

I have thought about this for a long time
and this is the conclusion I reached: salt and pepper

is a nice way of saying you are getting old.
I am actually the one who is getting old here.
You can tell by the piles of leaves I set on fire.
Not so much by what I say—there will always
be moments when some neat burst of spring

finds me saying something outlandish—but by
the manner in which I say I love you
to the men and women I know
passing through this life. Piles of leaves
are not sandwiches. We have established that
already. I am moving into the thickening place
where the gruel of blandishments
pushes me into inconstant theories
such as this—I want to kill John Milton

but he is already dead. Nonetheless I move;
timorously I move toward the great lettuce
of knowledge. There are various elements
involved and each one is another possible
chart. Thomas Merton is graph paper;
John Milton wrote incredible sonnets
about graph paper; there are melodies
about sandwiches; of the many golden melodies
in pain, perhaps I am the most sorrowful.
No one makes whoopee inside a bun.
The proof is in the flowers you press
in pages of your book at night. Thomas Merton died
with a hat pulled down over his penis.
It is not the way I want to die;
I want to die in a nice delicatessen
with all the lights off except for one,
the light on the bread. I would then
stand beside that light and read books.
If anything can slow the going into death
good light is probably that thing. John
Milton went blind. Thomas Merton
wrote letters from prison in the dark.

What did I ever write except for this note?
If you do not want to be my wife
I will understand. I wouldn't want
to marry someone so obsessed
he startles the wind into thistle.
Lettuce is only code for needing you.
Thomas Merton buried his sock under a tree
because he was incredibly sad.

# I Want an Empanada

I am in the middle of the plantain
I am leaning into the dresser
In the middle of the sculpture
I want an empanada
To slip through the grass
To settle my outstanding debts
I call upon the power company
I want an empanada
Bring me a clean towel
I need a napkin to be human
I could use a drink about now
To understand the sundown
I want an empanada
I cry into the wind
Dirt does not boil
I remove a potato from a pot
I cannot whistle to save myself
I want an empanada
But it never comes on time
I never come from anywhere
The potato disagrees
The town is getting bigger
The town is getting smaller
Someone threw a good ham
Out a bad window
And I felt the empathy
I had felt about the poor
Slide into another frame

# Hotel

*Lauren Shapiro*

I walk in only to find the 10th Annual
Chicago Bears Fan Convention.
My brain aches from the torment
of never aching like this before.
I came looking for peace but found a panel discussion
on the efficacy of jock straps.
Trickledown economics, do your work!
Spread your wings, Sweet Sue.
Blow your blowtorch, Angry Al.
Bastard Barb, keep crying into your napkins
and throwing them under the table. The pile is like
all the fans drinking beer and hugging each other
in the lobby. Light as a shadow of themselves they rise
to the 16th floor. They refill their ice buckets.
I'm in the hot tub when I get bumrushed
by Tank Johnson. He's wearing a speedo
designed by the Swedish military.
They have a military? I ask.
I just bumrushed you, says Tank Johnson.
Then he leaves to swim laps in the pool.
He's faster than I would have thought.

# If You Are Lost, Don't Move

They say hysteria leads to water loss.
That post-it note in your pocket could come in handy.
Always, the most important item in your purse
is the compact mirror. At the top of the pine tree
lies another pine tree, but this one's imagined
and too high to climb. Did I say *I love you*
when I left the house today?
If you remain stationary long enough, someone
will bump into you. If you are five years old
and pretend to disappear, you will be found.
Survival is relative in certain hemispheres
of the human brain. The recipe calls for
ten gallons of maple syrup and an ingredient
you've never heard of. You are alone.
You will have to scale a gorge you didn't know existed
and leave all of your keepsakes at the bottom of the well.
No one said it would be easy. Did you pack a defibrillator?
Are you aware of how many questions will need
to be answered? All around you, nature goes on
being nature in its subtle way. You call out *me*
and it spits back *me* in a thousand dipping leaves.
Go ahead, try to ask for help.
The clouds will be whatever shape you want
as they move past.

# A Hand

*Joe Fletcher*

I was in line in a café in winter, thinking about future appointments, obligations, tax shelters, the rash creeping across my daughter's armpit, the article in the magazine curled in my jacket pocket that I could perhaps finish over lunch, about the Pakistani terrorist camp discovered in cavernous bunkers drilled beneath rugged and treeless peaks, the time left on the meter. I was also whistling along with Rush's "Fly By Night," clutching my cell phone reassuringly and secretly inside my pants pocket, digesting breakfast, wondering if I should put some more food in me. The line was long and slow. I am an impatient man.

I glared reproachfully at the back of the man in front of me. I began to notice him: he was taller than me—and I am at least 6'4"—and wore a long greatcoat into the pockets of which his hands were stuffed, and a fedora hat over his bald, pale, fleshy head (only the back of which I could see). An intricate network of wrinkles formed in the basin where the back of his skull joined his neck. White iPod earphones were inserted into his enormous cauliflower ears, on which rested the stems of his dark sunglasses. What was he listening to? A woman's voice, reading softly from a Lithuanian novel about an aviator pursued by the ghost of the enemy pilot he shot down over the Black Forest? Or perhaps just a quiet wash of static punctuated by remote cries that could be birds, or schoolchildren trapped in a bus, slowly sinking into a Guatemalan canal?

Thinking maybe I would eat something, I perused the pastry case and its array of glazed and be-sprinkled dough, illuminated on glass shelves beneath harsh fluorescent glare. Something caught my eye that made my heart leap. On the bottom shelf, between a tray of lemon poppyseed muffins and a plate of pumpkinbread, was a human hand: cold, bloodless, pristine.

The nails were buffed and manicured, but it was beyond doubt a man's hand. A man's right hand. It rested on a paper doily upon a glass plate, palm down, fingers slightly bent, as if the hand were still connected to a man, face down, arm extended, dead, or relaxing. Some chocolate syrup had been drizzled carelessly around the rim of the plate—one rivulet traversed the thumb at its major knuckle.

Without thinking I reached for the hand, but was clumsily rebuffed by the thick glass pane of the pastry case. I blushed and quickly withdrew my hand back into my pocket, glancing behind me: no one. I continued to watch the hand out of the corner of my eye: it looked impossibly heavy, as if it was poised to crush—with its sheer weight—the plate, the shelf, the earth beneath it, plummeting out of this dimension and leaving a gaping, whistling hole behind it. But it remained. A steam wand hissed inside a foaming pitcher of milk. Beans were ground to a powder. A toddler burst out laughing from a rear table.

Then it was the turn of the man in front of me to order. He leaned stiffly toward the clerk, murmured his request, the pastry case door slid open, and I saw with horror the plate slide back and reappear on the counter beside the register, the hand looking slightly pale but unbruised in the open air. The man removed his left hand from his coat pocket and handed the clerk a Visa credit card. We waited, I in dread, the man in inscrutable silence, the clerk indifferently—his hair was braided in cornrows and he was humming along with Foreigner's "Double Vision," staring vacantly out over the patrons, his hand poised above the credit card receipt slit, which ejected a slip of paper, which the clerk read, frowned, and said: "Sorry, sir, but your card doesn't seem to be working," to which the man murmured an apology and produced, after some digging about in his left hand pocket with his left hand, a Mastercard. It worked.

The man removed himself to a corner window table and sat hunched over the hand, which rested on its plate, alone on the table. The man was motionless, his hands plunged in his coat pockets, his sunglasses reflecting the sun that penetrated the window. I stuttered out an order for a medium soy latté and sat at a table some distance from but facing the man, my magazine open and unread before me.

And we sat, the sands of the day sliding into the abyss. The commotion, the comings and goings of the patrons brushed against me like an unnoticed breeze as I watched him, discreetly. At certain moments I perceived a writhing within his pockets, as if something was forcibly trying to escape; and was he clenching his teeth, or was that just the set of his massive jaw? My cell phone began to agitate against my thigh, as my continued absence from my daily stations began to be noticed. I felt for the silver button with my thumb and silenced the machine each time it buzzed.

The afternoon deepened to dusk. The hand—to my gaze—grew soft, plump, tender, as my hunger grew. I dared not turn away from him, but as the night darkened I could no longer restrain the urge to urinate. I hurried to the bathroom—o agonizingly interminable stream—and returned to find the man, having exchanged the plate for a paper bag, pushing the glass door open and striding out into the night. I gathered my things and followed.

So it goes, from city to city. I am sure he is aware of my presence, my yellow Honda in his rearview mirror, my partially averted profile at the end of the buffet line, though he has not acknowledged me. He seems sometimes to linger, to drive more slowly, as if humoring my attempts at covert pursuit. He drives with his iPod inserted into his orifices. And I am waiting to make a move about which I remain uncertain. I write this from a Red Roof Inn near Milwaukee. It is March 12. I hear the interstate rushing beyond my window. And from the next room, when I press my ear to the vent, I hear skin being touched.

# Mercury Four

*Macgregor Card*

Gathering in speed is my advice
I'm ordering my charity to open
like a fine ammonia
passed on beast to beast
those animals

I'd know my family in broad daylight
I see clear to mercury at noon
wild oaks to fumigate
day owls to make
light of and gas out

teen veterans on speed, sabbatical
the day sabbatical, like I'd be writhing
on a fountain
on a day like this
not out there

coveting some ogre's wildcrafted denim
at the old folks prom, day prom
torrential day of rest
stay positive
not in the nude

but volunteered to grip the leather guide
to minerals in tartarus and almost read
look off, but quite almost read
can it be done ?

like what goes on
behind closed doors on new year's eve
under the table in broad daylight
honors me if I can handle it
Day I can handle it


I have an affirmation to confess
I'm earnest and it isn't even casual
I'm suddenly this ordinary man
I'm dressing for the vigil
I would rather hold

Almost the day is my advice
a father to me
how much harder do I have
to volunteer ?
does it get easier
to bring you to your knees
in laughter when I cripple you
with disappointment
waiting for an invitation
to go down?

places ? *glad to.* everybody here ?
let's nail it and slow down
let's nail it for a while)

Sit down at a table
made of oak in agony
and join your friends

Try walking like the animated statue
of someone humiliated
If you're honest with yourself
you'll be a natural, a friend
almost a *capability*
and in return
I want to be a natural with you
To easily look down, elect, as if all night
but in the beast of day
fan out in gaiety and anguish
and get seen
I love you to show up
so positively shine
so brighten up
a line of ruined chalk
under the weeds
look down that
sea of legs
Yeah hell there is
that line
So follow down
To love you
I'd be living to design
the ocean moving
only with its total heat
(your body's hard)
it's either only hard
or only hard for theater
you have material
for everyone, not me ?
(so why not me ?)

Take my ring, it's no baton, I hold it too

My whole ring, friends, I mean it
This is me now
and it's really fucking hard to interject—
                              you've all been someone
                              that I want to feel incredible
                              to know, and do, but then I also think
                              you're someone I could please so much
              it worries me, and even worse
                              you worry me just fine right now
it's awful—screwed-up torso clover
                              I can hear you like you're ordinary
                              growing down, a creaking violet
                              getting scarce, I hear you fine
                              I'm sorry, I'll get off

                              Still here, it's just that
                              friends are someone
              (maybe not platonically)
                              that I could really satisfy
                              if given just
                              one awful opportunity

                              *so horrible*

              shut up   *be cool*   go on

All morning in the sack on video ?
(might not)
I'm dim at being casual
to legendary movement
Day should be so
            indiscernible
erotic saddened mundo


eight mature irridiums at dusk



one minute you're a soda
burning through a pond that used to be
a dedicated fountain to great venuses, the best
and when you learn that
venus like a bear can scale a tree in search of prunes
you're totally an old, a liberal falcon
and a chevron made of
gold and barely titillating yarn
is on your shoulder
called the force
just left the building
and the country, left the pole
the wind that takes
            a vacant carabiner to the pole
at night, a favorite nudist chime, salute, that's all

Remember my physique
when I was that expedient
in reagan's second term?

My dickinson was varsity

My countenance was fey
My body would not quit
It will today

and honestly

a whistle has one note
that's all you get
it's unmistakable and chill

but you can

play it like a trumpet, mute
to anything you hear in faith
but cannot advocate

you can return

with total grievance
in the place of little banging
abject digs that, turning arch

with a controlled rotation

heat but won't commit

I have an affirmation
to confess

Who loves the way
        your heels scorch the earth
        down to its
        bright arena floor
        I do

Come watch
        the leaves go off with me
        at cape canaveral
        this fucking
        autumn ?

Earn a living in this house ?
        I do

The entire pit
of my receptacle
is Spirit—
I'm not young

Do I have heat ?

Prevail a little
closer to me
Is my stirring
excellent ?

Remember
my physique ?

But now
I'm ready

for the worm
of hygiene
and the feat
of strength

Just promise this—
Appeal to me
Okay ?  You'll just
Appeal to me ?

Once I can prefer
the blue face of the lord
to the red innumerable one
I'll be in heaven
w/ my cardiac indifference
I will finally perceive
my testicles as speech
I'd kill to be
that barely elevated

Ultimately plain

*Lewis Freedman*

D o (g)   r o t (s)   m (y) ( aim ) ( by )
s o (f (tening) ( the ) ( brisket )
w o (rds)   b i n (ge)   o (ver)   ( s) o (da)
a (nd)   o n e    r a (ises)   l (id)
w (e)   ( cel (i (bates)   ( to )   b o (ot)
a (rchive)   a v (e - maria)   g (in)
l o (ads)   a r e    g o (ne)   ( and )
( pi  c (k)    r e (volve)   ( lin (t)
( populates )   ( a )   t (ry)   ( and )
( mar (s)   ( error )   ( like )   ( a (s)
l o (se)   t ( r (yst)   ( we ('d)   r (ipped)
( a )   ( n e w (t)   ( a )   ( newt )
( a (n)   g i (st)   ( of f   ( a )   s (ynd -
icate)   r o o (m)   ( across )   t (in)
( water )   t r u (st)   ( eeking )
l o (ne)   g (host)   w i l (ly)
( boyd )   a s (teroid)
( ins (ular)   ( in )   ( a (r (t)   g o (verns)
a (rc)   o (r)   s e (cludes)   ( line )
w (ith)   o (ve (n)   c l o (ves)   ( on )
( goo (n)   ( g (ov)   a s   ( we )
t (rain)   ( to )   ( be )   ( g o (ds)
i n (to)   p o (verty)   ( adjustment )
w (in (ners)   ( and )   ( dr (y)   o (ctagons)
( on (e)   a r (c)   ( at )   ( two )   ( timings )

[Note: This poem is of a notational method of writing in which I begin attempting to make words at the speed and shape of letter without a word in mind. If I can get to the end of the word I am spelling without producing the word in my mind, the word appears without parenthesis but with spaces between each letter [a r e]. If the word is heard in mind prior to the end of the letter-making and I am forming letters into the already known word, I notate with parentheses from the heard point until the end of the word [l o (ner)]. If the entire word is unavoidably heard before I begin to form its first letter I notate in full parenthesis [( brigadier )]. Other occurrences in the poem are extensions of this notational logic, e.g. I begin a word having already heard it but it changes in the letter forming and is notated like this: ( so (lar).]

# (16) Your Health

One of the most usual poses to bear soluble time through the sentences, I consistently assert like I begin in some counterpart of loss that's anything other than begotten plot ... far be it from me meets the mail thing with miles to shore. The dispute is age arranging the face at what is recognized as surface ... trying ... to find fault with the millions of your replenishing ... directed against those who found fault with the left memory scribbles replaying: one to cheat for five. I'm accusing a title of having created worlds that slander the memory of the serpent (or 'duration hose')'s famous saying. He found he was ready to make all the trees place a double bearing in the stolen mind ... very often now the indistinguishable is anonymously the sane. I see this sermon staring at the surface of the pho. What do ye want with food? Go and title a trouble for your contemporaries ... supplying you with moves on their antennas' behalves. Evidence: gadfly to the maxim ... evidence the failings of the maxim to supply more than an implied politics for its abundantly mangled severity supply. Surely this is directed together with an erasure in the present: stir up my honor ... before my honor ... my honor is nothing ... before the honor of my honor. Descending in the dialogue there to be magnified ... Rat 1: I'm which I try to remain ... to anticipate the real is ... not in agony it is agony ... Tim: I'm quoting the inducing team here ... if I went with them ... what good can I be ... to them ... beguiled by notice of a spark ... I'm like ... is this an official spark ... you can tell ... if the speaking at the edges is louder than the gut ... Top: Leave him alone ... he's like a scribe who didn't rise early to go to the roof alone ... and engage in the dilemma of being ... trapped in first meeting ... sky in the difference between ... hanging out on a roof and jumping out off a roof ... and now he wants to be punished.

[from *Residual Synonyms for the Name of God*.]

# ALVERTA

*Kiki Petrosino*

Say she was noble: a bright & foreign kind. Her long-gloved hands, her

smell of coins & salt. She had a way of staring over the yokes of trees at

you. Slim, in her woven skirt & church heels. All that light hair twisting

through a comb like speech. Now say the railroad came & changed the

whole county. Railroad came & slithered over the mountains to where you

can't catch. Tobacco in the lungs, grease unfolding in the mouth. How,

year by year, your father's voice grew narrow & sweet with graves. *Clifton*,

he called you. *Butler-William-Henry.* Called you to the home-place

where God Himself slept like a spine in the earth. But say you kissed her,

once: a taste of glass. Say she muttered over you. Grandfather of smoke,

grandfather of great sorrow. Tell us what you gave for all the stars drowned

in her skin. For her womanish back of the neck, tilting away.

# Farm 2

*Paul Legault*

The contract began somewhat sporadically
Involving the land animals' removal of their others
While keeping a few agents at hand
To bridge one thing from another.
Our status felt unnatural.
We drew a force from the property
Of course, but that didn't mean anything
When it came to be about an emotional attachment
To the physical partition that exists
Uninjured by sight and our sudden escape plans.

So we left the city for once
In a steadfast manner with the new girl
Who established that white fences exist
And that the comings and goings could
Do just that. Poppies and irises
Negate them. The purple of the ages
Calls for you, wretchedly. Few enough
Get by, but this was their season
With you amongst them. There was one
Who hadn't been excused to be there.

# Farm II 2

Now that they've found
Another use for ferns
       that they'd forgot about
They'll grow foreign in the public world
That gently houses our militia.
One product of memory associated itself
With the blue documents
The tinmaker'd drawn up. Frontiers
Can't adjust to their errors. The study room
Fills up with boys,

And there was some information available,
But mostly we came to
Simultaneously in a position
Of grace, with one leg asleep.

I signed up for
A time at the center.
I would've liked to prepare myself

Prior to this evening's lattice-work
Was constructed across the road
To distinguish the children through it
From the forestry they ravaged
In becoming that indecorous sort
Of workmen of the departing carriages
    of a burnt umber.
They whistled all at once, though the temple was closed
And thus the proposal along with it

Which had been for the time being.
But nothing doesn't fumble
Or make a likeness.

# Farm III 2

There are little versions of water
That attack you
Irreversibly in a motion
Given to them, the final sibilants,
And then to you among them.

What was dark was the fluidity of these situations
And of the oils they used to replace them.
Surely we'd have composed ourselves
In another time just as wildly
Extravagant if also suddenly
As a mouse's lisp.
The fractions reflect their other numbers
And the fecundity of a whole
Put into us. Carry off your answers
Into the harmony of these two bridges
As if catapulted from a previous assignment.

# CUBE

*Lidija Dimkovska*

I removed one side of the cube
and got a box to keep books or toys in,
I kept my amputated arm in it, my severed head,
and my viscera with wax seals.
I removed two sides of the cube
and here I am with a trailer to stretch my legs into infinity
a lectern without a lecture that I used for
my first steps, my last fall.
I removed three sides of the cube
and it became a table for my elbow,
a personal tunnel for my red flesh,
a gate to the moment I was begotten, a shroud
under which I crawl as if under the grave of life.
Four sides off and it's a shack,
a night-time pyramid, a tent for two,
a sail for a storm, a shelter for death.
I removed five sides of the cube and got a mirror,
a self-portrait, freedom with corrections,
a white pillow, a sheet of black paper.
I watched over the sixth side and caressed it,
sweetie, sweetie I was saying to it,
it was a pretty square with accurate angles of 90°.
I protected it from everything alien to it,
I hid it from everything that was strange to it,
I became its glass dome, bulletproof glass,
curled up with my arms on the floor
to become one with it,
but instead of being resurrected as a cube

—I broke, exploded, and the cleaner came
and swept the shards up in her dustpan,
wiped out my shadow with a damp cloth
and closed the door. The cube cubed me.

*Translated from the Macedonian by Ljubica Arsovska and Peggy Reid.*

# POEM AS MIRROR BOX: MIRROR NEURONS, EMOTIONS, PHANTOM LIMBS, AND POEMS OF LOSS AND ELEGY

*Lee Ann Roripaugh*

Considered one of the most exciting and significant discoveries in neuroscience, mirror neurons are neurons located in "key parts of our brains—the premotor cortex and centers for language, empathy and pain—and fire not only as we perform a certain action but when we watch someone else perform that action" (Dobbs 22). Mirror neurons not only explain a lot about how our bodies learn to perform both simple and complex physical tasks, but are also crucial with respect to our emotional and psychosocial functioning—*i.e.*, how we read the emotions of others, develop empathy, and learn to identify and process our own emotional states. In a 2006 article for *Scientific American Mind*, science writer David Dobbs noted that: "At a deeper level, [mirror neurons suggest] a biological dynamic for our understanding of others, the complex exchange of ideas we call culture, and psychosocial dysfunctions ranging from lack of empathy to autism. Comprehending mirror neurons helps us make sense of why yawns are contagious to why, watching Olivier fall to his knees, we feel Hamlet's grief for Ophelia" (24).

Attributing mirror neurons and imitation learning as the source of the "great leap forward" in human evolution, V. S. Ramachandran, one of the scientists at the forefront of studies in mirror neurons, has claimed that "[ . . . ] mirror neurons will do for psychology what DNA did for biology: they will provide a unifying framework and help explain a host of mental abilities that have hitherto remained mysterious and inaccessible to experiments" (Ramachandran, "Mirror Neurons and Imitation Learning as the Driving Force Behind the 'Great Leap Forward' in Human Evolution"). Hailed by Sandra Blakeslee in a 2006 *New York Times* article as "Cells That Read Minds," mirror neurons enable us to analyze scenes in order to distinguish intent (Blakeslee). They guide us in making the cognitive distinctions by which we determine whether someone is picking up a glass to drink from it, or picking up a glass in order to begin clearing a table, or picking up a glass to throw a drink in our face (Dobbs 26). One of the original team members who first discovered mirror neurons at the University of Parma in 1991, Dr. Giacomo Rizzolatti, framed the significance of this discovery primarily in terms of its emotional and social implications. Rizzolatti stated, "We are exquisitely social creatures [ . . . ]. Our survival depends on understanding the actions, intentions and emotions of others. [ . . . ] Mirror neurons allow us to grasp the minds of others not through conceptual reasoning but through direct simulation. By feeling, not by thinking" (Blakeslee).

This application has been consistently borne out by scientists such as Dr. Christian Keysers, who studies the neurological implications of empathy at the University of Groningen in the Netherlands and discovered that the ability to share the emotions of others is intimately linked to mirror neurons. Interestingly enough, people who test high on a psychological scale registering empathy have particularly active mirror neuron systems. According to Dr. Keysers, social emotions like guilt, shame, pride, embarrassment, disgust, and lust are based on a uniquely human mirror neuron system found in a part of the brain called the insula. In his experiments, Dr. Keysers found that when people watched a hand go forward to caress someone and then saw another hand push it away rudely, the insula registered the social pain of rejection, indicating that social emotions such as humiliation are mapped in the brain by the same mechanisms that encode real physical pain (Blakeslee).

Fascinating, yes, but what do mirror neurons have to do with poetry? Intriguingly, one of the most active sites of mirror neuron systems is located in the "Broca's area," an area of the brain crucial to language processing. In 1998, Dr. Michael Arbib, a neuroscientist at the University of Southern California, discovered that language itself appears to rise from the same syntactic understanding of action generated by our mirror neurons. Furthermore, in 2005, experiments conducted by Drs. Gallese and Rizzolatti of the original Parma team indicated that when people listen to sentences describing actions, the same mirror neurons fire that would fire if the people had been either performing the actions described, or visually witnessing the actions being described (Dobbs 25). The implications for this in terms of both considering and reconsidering how writers and readers both create and respond to language—in particular, poetry—seem fabulously rich. For example, by specifically focusing on the research conducted by V. S. Ramachandran regarding mirror neurons and phantom limbs, one can begin to make a number of very interesting connections between neuroscience and poetry—thereby arriving at new ways of thinking about the neurocognitive and affective functions of poems of loss and elegy.

V. S. Ramachandran's well-known work with mirror neurons and phantom limb syndrome revealed that brain maps are not fixed or static, as originally thought, but are highly malleable, and can reorganize or reconfigure themselves in response to the loss of a limb. Many patients who have lost an arm or leg continue to feel the presence of the limb in their brain—a condition known as "phantom limb" syndrome—and in some cases, the phantom limb may be fixed, or paralyzed, in an excruciatingly painful cramped position. Ramachandran speculated that this state of painful paralysis continued because when patients attempted to move the phantom limb, their brains received sensory feedback—from visual perception and proprioception—that, because the limb was missing, the phantom limb was paralyzed and could not move. This feedback, over time and repetition, would imprint itself further into the brain circuitry so that the brain, through a process of Hebbian learning, came to "know" that the missing limb (and the phantom limb) was paralyzed (Ramachandran and Blakeslee, 52–55).

Ramachandran theorized that this knowledge of paralysis in the phantom limb could be unlearned, however, through delivering an alternate set of visual information to the patients' brains. With this in mind, Ramachandran created a mirror box, in which mirrors were used in such a way that a mirror reflection of an amputee patients' intact arm was optically superimposed on the felt location of the patient's phantom arm—thereby creating the visual illusion that the phantom arm was now once again resurrected and embodied. When patients were then told to move their intact, existing hands out of the paralyzed, cramped position while looking at this optical illusion, they not only saw the phantom limb move, but also *felt* the phantom limb move. Astonishingly, this seemed to cure the paralysis and pain in some of the phantom limb patients, while in other patients, the phantom limb disappeared altogether, along with the pain (Ramachandran and Blakeslee, 46–49).

Along similar lines, when patients witnessed their phantom limbs being touched (also using the optical illusion with the mirror box), they sometimes experienced touch sensations in the phantom limb. And to take this even one step further, Ramachandran found that patients with phantom limbs also experienced the sensation of touch in their phantom limbs when they witnessed someone else's intact limb being rubbed—so much so, that pain in the phantom limb could be relieved through this neural, empathetic reading of another person's sensory experience (Ramachandran and Blakeslee, 58–62).

Given the emotional and linguistic significance of mirror neurons as outlined above, it seems reasonable to suggest that emotional losses and psychological traumas might function somewhat analogously to the physical trauma of limb loss and the concomitant neurocognitive "haunting" by a phantom limb. In fact, Maurice Merleau-Ponty, in 1945's *Phenomenology of Perception*, makes a philosophical connection between these elements that uncannily seems to adumbrate the neurocognitive connections gleaned from the study of mirror neurons. Comparing phantom limb syndrome to the loss of a friend or dear one, Merleau-Ponty writes: "We do not understand the absence or death of a friend until the moment we expect a reply from him and realize there will never be one" (93). For Merleau-Ponty, emotional intelligence and phantom limb are both types of "preconscious knowledge," and he goes on to state that "memory, emotion, and phantom limb are equivalents with regard to being in the world" (99).

Consider, for example, the losses that haunt many of Li-Young Lee's poems and, in particular, his poem "The Hour and What is Dead." Like phantom limb syndrome, these hauntings are uncanny. They create unnerving, even painful or burning, physical images and sensations for the speaker of the poem:

> Tonight my brother, in heavy boots, is walking
> through bare rooms over my head,
> opening and closing doors.
> What could he be looking for in an empty house?
> What could he possibly need there in heaven?
> Does he remember his earth, his birthplace set to torches?
> His love for me feels like spilled water
> running back to its vessel.
>
> At this hour, what is dead is restless
> and what is living is burning.
>
> Someone tell him he should sleep now.

My father keeps a light on by our bed
and readies for our journey.
He mends ten holes in the knees
of five pairs of boy's pants.
His love for me is like sewing:
various colors and too much thread,
the stitching uneven. But the needle pierces
clean through with each stroke of his hand.

At this hour, what is dead is worried
and what is living is fugitive.

Someone tell him he should sleep now.

God, that old furnace, keeps talking
with his mouth of teeth,
a beard stained at feasts, and his breath
of gasoline, airplane, human ash.
His love for me feels like fire,
feels like doves, feels like river-water.

At this hour, what is dead is helpless, kind
and helpless. While the Lord lives.

Someone tell the Lord to leave me alone.
I've had enough of his love
that feels like burning and flight and running away (35–6).

My question, then, is that if language has the ability to empathetically
trigger mirror neurons, and if an emotional loss or psychological trauma
(such as the death of a loved one) can be in any way construed as being
neurocognitively similar to the loss of an appendage and the subsequent

phantom limb syndrome, is it possible to suggest that poems of loss and elegies are the emotional and artistic equivalents of Ramachandran's mirror boxes?

Furthermore, is it possible that the elegiac poem as mirror box projects an artistic illusion upon the phantom limb of the loss/trauma, either through reanimating a lost beloved or reanimating a psychological trauma, in a way that returns agency over the trauma for the poem's speaker—thereby allowing the brain to *unlearn* the traumatic paralysis of loss, so to speak, so that the phantom limb of this loss might uncramp from its state of excruciating emotional pain and paralytic trauma?

With this background in mind, another lens by which to read the affective processes of a poem of loss emerges, but even more intriguingly, a number of poems seem to *ritually enact* Ramachandran's mirror box process in surprisingly explicit terms. For example, when thinking of potential mirror box poems, one of the first that might come to mind is Anne Sexton's poem, "For John, Who Begs Me Not to Enquire Further," with its built-in mirroring between the speaker and the apostrophic "you" in the poem, as well as the evocation of stars as metaphors for poems. Written to her mentor, John Holmes, who emphatically recommended Sexton *not* publish the poems which eventually constituted *To Bedlam and Part Way Back*, the poem is frequently cited as Sexton's defense for the confessional aesthetic. Well aware that Holmes, who lost his own wife to suicide, was suffering from his own traumas and griefs—ones that may have made him particularly vulnerable to being troubled by her work—Sexton arguably creates a symbolic mirror box in the poem. One in which the speaker of the poem sits face-to-face with the "you" in the poem, ostensibly John Holmes, mirroring and empathetically connecting speaker and reader in gazing together upon the mediating glass bowl of cracked stars that is the poem. The closing lines read:

And if you turn away
because there is no lesson here
I will hold my awkward bowl,
with all its cracked stars shining
like a complicated lie,
and fasten a new skin around it
as if I were dressing an orange
or a strange sun.
Not that it was beautiful,
but that I found some order there.
There ought to be something special
for someone
in this kind of hope.
This is something I would never find
in a lovelier place, my dear,
although your fear is anyone's fear,
like an invisible veil between us all . . .
and sometimes in private,
my kitchen, your kitchen,
my face, your face (34).

Here, the speaker creates a mirror image by which traumatic autobiographical experience is reanimated, but then palindromically transformed into something of potential use or value, much in the same way that Sexton's favorite palindrome transformed RATS into STARS.

This idea of poem as mirror box is also ritually enacted in Yusef Komunyakaa's well-known poem, "Facing It," in which the speaker of the poem, a black veteran, observes himself, as well as other veterans and visitors, reflected in the black granite of the Vietnam Veterans Memorial. The granite is static and unyielding, its 58,022 names representative of incomprehensible loss and trauma at both personal and cultural levels—a memorial in which these personal and cultural traumas can be thought of as a phantom limb frozen in painful paralysis. The speaker sees himself fade into the stone. He feels surprised that he doesn't see his own name there. He also observes a white veteran, who has, interestingly, "lost his arm / inside the stone" (159). Rather than remaining permanently trapped or paralyzed within this trauma, however, in the same way that phantom limbs are visually reanimated by Ramachandran's mirror boxes, the optical illusion created by the living, intact people reflected upon the phantom limb of the memorial restores movement to that which is static, cramped, and grieving. Veterans and visitors—all who have lost something within the stone—see themselves alive and in motion, and are thereby able to move forward and initiate a ritual of mourning: "Names shimmer on a woman's blouse / but when she walks away / the names stay on the wall." Or, at the conclusion of the poem: "In the black mirror / a woman's trying to erase names. / No, she's brushing a boy's hair" (159).

Another particularly explicit instance of poem as mirror box is performed in Anne Carson's most recent book, *Nox*, constructed as an elegy for her dead brother. *Nox* is book as art object: an epitaph, a scroll, a collage of photographs, letters, fragments, and poetry that acknowledges a survival around an incomprehensible absence—an absence that cannot be got round, or captured, but is nonetheless painstakingly reassembled, despite this incomprehensibility, into the literal mirror box of the book, much in the same way that Anne Carson, as a Greek Classicist, reassembles extant fragments of ancient text, or recovers and retranslates the lexicography of words.

> 1.2 Autopsy is a term historians use of the "eyewitnessing" of data or events by the historian himself, a mode of authorial power. To withhold this authorization is also powerful. [ . . . ]When my brother died his dog got angry, stayed angry, barking, growling, lashing, glaring, by day and night. He went to the door, he went to the window, he would not lie

down. My brother's widow, it is said, took the dog to the church on the day of the funeral. Buster goes right up to the front of Sankt Johannes and raises himself on his paws on the edge of the coffin and as soon as he smells the fact, his anger stops. "To be nothing—is that not, after all, the most satisfactory fact in the whole world?" asks a dog in a novel I read once (Virginia Woolf, *Flush*, 87). I wonder what the smell of nothing is. Smell of autopsy (15).

Several pages later, she writes:

> [ . . . ] In cigarette-smoke-soaked Copenhagen, under a wide thin sorrowful sky, as swans drift down the water, I am looking a long time into the muteness of my brother. It resists me. He refuses to be "cooked" (a modern historian might say) in my transactional order. To put this another way, there is something that facts lack. "Overtakelessness" is a word told me by a philosopher once: das Unumgangliche—that which cannot be got round. Cannot be avoided or seen to the back of. And about which one collects facts—it remains beyond them (17).

In the concluding pages of the book, the image of the brother, which uncannily haunts the text like the phantom limb syndrome described by Ramachandran, eerily appears in the stairwell, and then simply disappears.

*He refuses, he is in the stairwell, he disappears* (189).

The remainder of the text in the book is illegible.

Another interesting instance of poem as mirror box could arguably be found in Sylvia Plath's poem "Mirror." Here, however, the loss appears to be one of agency, or power. The mirror in the poem is silver, exact, and controlling. It gazes, judges, and speaks. It reflects the woman with its scopophilic gaze, inscribing values of idealized female beauty, youth, and worth onto her static image. The woman is paralyzed with loss of agency and loss of voice/self under the pressures of this patriarchal gaze. However, a small flutter of movement, or protest, is finally projected upon this loss of agency—"tears" and an "agitation of hands" (174). And by the end of the poem, the passive girl, trapped within the narrow confines of the mirror's judgmental gaze, has drowned in these exacting standards to be replaced by a frightening older woman, "a terrible fish," rising from the silver depths (174). This new woman does not conform to the narrow confines of cultural standards for female beauty. Yet "this terrible fish" is now liberated and mobile. She is monstrous, potentially transgressive, and comparatively powerful.

As an interesting twist on this notion of poem as mirror box, it could be suggested that poems which wrestle with anxieties surrounding science and technology, ideas of the post-human, and postmodern nostalgia in an age of mechanical reproduction might, within the mirror box analogy, arguably create an optical illusion of an intact *prosthetic* limb superimposed over the paralyzed, phantom limb within the poem's mirror box—both as a means of reifying these perceived losses and anxieties, as well as simultaneously exploring their transgressive potentials. Take Susan Slaviero's poem, "Robosexual," for example, from her collection of cyborg feminist poems, *Cyborgia*:

> The unwritten eggs beneath her veil,
> aluminum legbones, a locust husk,
> the embroidery of her threaded tongue.
> I allow for flux, fissure,
> for saints kneeling on upturned spoons.
> This scene is about design.
>
> Later, under girl-cheek moons,
> she drizzles spittle on a man's abdomen.

The poppies on her helmet disguise
starlike dents, a row of rivets. Wake up
and bend in unexpected ways.
A needle is warmed in the glimmer
of a kitchen match. You might be lulled
by the cut of her jaw, the unwinding
of her limbs. You might be hooked
on rubber dolls. You might be licking
your own reflection (11).

In "Robosexual" the cyborg woman functions as an empty signifier. She is the ultimate consumer commodity fetish object—all postmodern surface, entirely constructed, and utterly uncanny in her animation. She manifests as the product of a terrible yearning or nostalgia for the Real—one, however, that only leads the consumer back to the desires of the self ("you might be licking your own reflection"). Like Morpheus, the god of dreams, she wears a crown of poppies over her "starlike dents," and so despite her clever design, we are reminded that she is merely simulacra, an illusion. Likewise, "Robosexual" can't help but underscore the constructed and performative nature of gender, along with the cultural nostalgia and yearnings that insist on repeatedly manufacturing these illusions of gender. In the end, like all female cyborgs, the cyborg in "Robosexual," with her "row of rivets," her "threaded tongue," and "unwritten eggs beneath her veil," ultimately emerges as uncanny, disturbing, monstrous—in short, a site of volatile and transgressive potential.

And finally, in the poem "Bardo" by Tibetan poet Tsering Wangmo Dhompa, the personal and communal loss of an "uncle who is no more" is ritualized not so much as trauma, or mourning, but as a guiding through the time in between death and rebirth understood, in the Tibetan Book of the Dead, as Bardo. Like the phantom limb, the uncle in Bardo is in a liminal, disembodied, uncanny space. If the uncle retains his concentration, learned in life through meditation, and does not become distracted, or paralyzed, by painful hallucinations, he has the possibility to learn from the state of Bardo, as well as ultimately move toward a positive transformation into someone or something new. The intact living people, through the mirror box of the poem, project a smooth voyage through the phantom limb state of Bardo, using language, memory, prayer, and ritual to help the uncle make this lovely transition:

A hundred and one butter lamps are offered to my uncle who is no more.

Distraction proves fatal in death. A curtain of butter imprints in air.

After the burning of bones, ashes are sent on pilgrimage. You are dead, go into life, we pray. My uncle was a man given to giggles in solemn moments.

Memory springs like crocuses in bloom. Self conscious and precise.

Without blurring the cornea, details are resuscitated. Dried yak meat between teeth. Semblance of what is.

Do not be distracted, Uncle who is no more.

He does not see his reflection in the river. The arching of speech over "s" as he is becoming.

Curvature of spine as it racked on a misty morning. A shadow evades the wall.

You are no more, Uncle who is no more.

Every seven days he must relive his moment of expiration. The living pray frequently amid burning juniper.

Communication efforts require the right initiative.

Somewhere along the line matters of motion and rest are resolved.

Crows pick the last offerings. You are someone else, uncle no more (62).

Clearly, these are all poems that appear to explicitly enact, through language, the recuperative processes of Ramachandran's mirror box—*i.e.*, illusions of reanimation across the surface of paralytic, crippling, and/or haunting traumas as a means of allowing the brain to reconceptualize, relearn, retransition, and move forward. It doesn't seem like too far a stretch, however, to suggest that perhaps *every* poem is a mirror box of sorts. Imagine our mirror neurons, lit up and flickering like glittery circuit boards, in mirrored response to every poem that we read. Indeed, the implications of mirror neurons, with respect to the ways in which we think about how we read and make poems, seems profound. Perhaps a poem teaches the brain, through language, things that are beyond the body's comprehension. Perhaps—at least on the neurocognitive level—poetry really *does* make things happen, after all.

# Works Cited

Blakeslee, Sandra. "Cells That Read Minds." *NYTimes.com*. The New York Times Company, 10 Jan. 2006. Web. 9 Feb. 2012.

Carson, Anne. *Nox*. New York: New Directions, 2010. Print.

Dhompa, Tsering Wangmo. "Bardo." *Rules of the House*. Berkeley: Apogee, 2002. Print.

Dobbs, David. "A Revealing Reflection." *Scientific American Mind*. Apr./May 2006: 22-27. Print.

Komunyakaa, Yusef. "Facing It." *Neon Vernacular: New and Selected Poems*. Hanover, NH: Wesleyan UP, 1993. Print.

Lee, Li-Young. "The Hour and What Is Dead." *The City in Which I Love You*. Rochester, NY: BOA, 1990. Print.

Merleau-Ponty, Maurice. *Phenomenology of Perception*. Trans. C. Smith. London and New York: Routledge, 2002. Print.

Plath, Sylvia. "Mirror." *The Collected Poems*. New York: Harper Perennial, 1981. Print.

Ramachandran, V. S. and Sandra Blakeslee. *Phantoms in the Brain*. New York: Harper Perennial, 1998. Print.

Ramachandran, V. S. "Mirror Neurons and Imitation Learning as the Driving Force Behind the 'Great Leap Forward' in Human Evolution." *Edge*. Edge Foundation, 31 May 2000. Web. 9 Feb. 2012.

Sexton, Anne. "To John, Who Begs Me Not to Enquire Further." *The Complete Poems: Anne Sexton*. New York: Mariner, 1999. Print.

Slaviero, Susan. "Robosexual." *Cyborgia*. Woodstock, NY: Mayapple Press, 2010. Print.

# CLOWN, GRIMACER, FLOORMAT, YESMAN, ENTERTAINER

*Elaine Kahn*

Oh you swimming public
be a friend
swish that public
slide again
your public dorsal white things
on the muggy
sedan floor

Trash is power
trash is open
is my field is
I feel
dirty in your eyes
yet indivisible our fat

Saying you are good
is not the same as being good
but is it proof that I don't love you

All you men of no good feeling
be forewarned
your animals resent you
they clench their jaws
& call their moms
so many times a day

# BE A FRIEND

Fortune faked you
snuck you from the dinner table, silent as a fold
how red your face
is raw meat red

Your carved-in Appalachian Becky voice
Becky, I have never talked in mine

When you are still
eleven, Becky
two hot bruises
when you shake
your hair
has never been more sure
and you are nearly old

You think beauty
is a good thing
to forgive

Just because
your parents had you, Becky
had to so you wouldn't have to
have you, with your shirt pulled up
the thumb print pressed
the tv red
if you are lucky, Becky
I will make you feel like you are lucky

Your smile like a finger

What is pleasing to me
is what I cannot mind

# Andy Warhol

*Mary Hickman*

Andy only wants to be told about his body by others. Like if I
am on the phone with him, standing here completely naked,
looking at my stretch marks. If, right now, I am looking at the
scar on my side from my abscessed breastbone and I am looking
at the scar on my leg from where I fell in the garden, he asks,
"What about *my* scars? What are they proof of?" Andy is all
eye—air and desert. Or he is inward illumination. This silence
of flesh, if it is the essence of Andy, is also the image we make
from his scars, his blisters, craters, pocks, and scabs. Often we
arrive at the point at which the Andy I offer the viewer, and
offer back to Andy, creases or buckles. It curls in humidity,
becomes rigid and vulnerable, loses flexibility. It's not that
I can't imagine Andy's abdomen alongside my own scarred
chest, but I remember reading how embarrassed he was in the
hospital. He started to collect things. The nuns encouraged
him to collect stamps. Coins, too. He never wants to bring his
personal life into his work in a direct way. It should never be
read as, "I'm telling you about my personal life, my friends,
this is what happened." I'd never go to Andy to understand
flesh, to think about these bodies, but if I wanted to know,
say, about quilts, about whether or not this is a real American
quilt, or if this Christmas was a real American Christmas, a
magazine Christmas, I'd ask Andy. Ask, are these Levis, not
just bluejeans? And of course he'd know. "I want to die with
my bluejeans on," and all that. The stitching involved in my
portrait of Andy—in order to distance the needle, in order to
get at not the skin not the stitching but capture what we feel as
we notice the expression he wears in the Avedon photo when

he lifts his shirt for us—embroidery is not painting, even if it seems to be. I did not invent embroidery, but as a maniacal and obsessive skill expanding over time, to sew flesh—to work in a field that teaches you to close wounds—is to work without emotion, shadowy. Andy does not possess a dynamic glance but one that is fixed, immobile, myopic in the rigidity of its stitching. He had a nightmare. He was taken to a clinic. He dreamed of a charity to cheer up people who were horribly disfigured, people who had to wear plastic across their faces and underneath there was nothing. We had this nightmare together or it was his nightmare alone but he repeated it so often it is now nearly a memory. "When the alcohol is dry," he says, "I am ready to apply the flesh-colored paint that doesn't resemble any human flesh I've ever seen, though it does come pretty close to mine." As a child, I visited the Great Wall. As a child I rode trains through the Gobi desert. As a child I wanted nothing more than bluejeans. The yellow crust of the Gobi, the olive uniforms of the guards, each stone of the wall the size of my leg and the steps in places impassable. What I realize, what the image of Andy reveals to Andy, is that his scars do not describe engrossing stories, do not stimulate indecent cravings; they do not excite. The same figures repeat in bands or clusters, stitched with the tailings gathered in knots, drawn in bundles, obscuring the chest or connecting it as lines of communication. When Andy looks in the mirror, when he is nothing and with no sense of existence, I am sure I'm going to look in the mirror and see nothing. People are always calling Andy a mirror and if a mirror looks into a mirror what is there to see? When the sun extracts the last drop of moisture from the skin, the skin shrinks, forms intricate patterns. When the heat cracks the chest, it draws salt, covering the chest in a fine web of seams. This is what we call a contemporary landscape. *Still-life and*

*Desire.* You were just lying there and I was standing over you crying. You kept telling me not to make you laugh, it really hurt. "And . . . ? And . . . ?" he asks. He will not stop asking. If someone else talks about it, I listen, I hear the words, and I think maybe it's all true. What about *your* scars, I say. I'll tell you about your scars. You put them to work for you. They're the best thing you have. These bodies, this molten mass of bodies constantly seething and circulating, forming cracks in the dark, cooled skin over the glowing image of Andy. It enables me to be happy with this piece, to sweeten the figure of Andy, to allow him to remain as he insists upon remaining: suspended in a vaporous narrative. We dissolve desire to enter the heart of Andy. There are bones in the Great Wall. My finger finds a finger-bone. There are wrists in this wall. And a pelvis, a pelvis is a fossil.

[Note: This poem adapts phrases from Andy Warhol's *The Philosophy of Andy Warhol: from A to B and back again* (Harcourt Books, 1975).]

# I Have Had Many Near-Death Experiences

Watching Kazuo Ohno dancing *Mother* I end up thinking, *oh mama mama, my turtledove.* Only fairytales come to mind. The song in "The Juniper Tree" sung by the murdered son become a bird: "My mother she killed me / My father he ate me / My sister Marlene gathered my bones / Tied them in a scarf / Laid them beneath the juniper tree." In *Mother,* when the music stops, the spotlight widens to reveal an audience perfectly stilled. It sounds as if Kazuo calls up North Sea winds from every direction, calls up a landscape of ragged cliffs and swells. Kazuo's rawness must be the rawness of the sea. He renders each pulsating twisting move of jellyfish in dance. How alien human figures can become. He has seen thousands of jellies circling victims of hunger or disease, soldiers buried at sea, men he knew in the war. He was a prisoner of war. Tuesday was yesterday, but today is Wednesday. They confirmed Wednesday that he died Tuesday. Is Tuesday in Japan Wednesday here? In *Mother,* the gestures are not eroticism, not desire, but percussive violence. He stamps ankles into strength. The dance demands he unlearn his upright body, unlock shoulder from spine, disarticulate each confined, trained joint. In Butoh, bodies distort beyond etiquette and beyond beauty, becoming crippled ships, bent forest floor. He must unfold his body, loosen the face and prepare for a face made utterly unrecognizable. Tracking his own corpse, he finds a face so fixed even agony cannot be found there. He dances the sharp chirping of insects, the animal's lowing, and thus unmoors his body. People say many things about Kazuo's body. It is a corpse standing, an outcry from somewhere beyond the culture of flesh. I find working from life so intimidating—I find it hard to do. I have had many near-death experiences, moments when I certainly might have died. On a mountain road near Taiwan's north coast, I bent over a cliff-edge to pick flowers and fell thirty feet. When I looked up, my companion gestured for me to stay still. He was yelling, *Don't move!* I moved and felt my body drop six inches. Only branches supported me and, below, the cliff dropped into mist. As Kazuo builds a dance, it's like adding layers of flesh. I hesitate to create a myth about Kazuo since we have to continue his endeavors. He needed a recipient. We had to be receptive. There is a moment when the image starts to breathe. There is something unsettled about the image, like form passing into a gesture that is *live*. Eight ghostly-white bodies emerge from the sea and scramble over the rocks. They move sideways over the sharp rocks, their soles splitting. They unfurl long red ribbons from their mouths like a secret, something that words can't touch. Exploring caves underwater, squeezing through smaller and smaller openings but always sure there would be another opening ahead, I was diving without equipment. I saw the reef and a school of squid just beyond. When my lungful of air began to run out, I tried to surface, and I saw a hole in the rock leading up. As I swam, the opening narrowed. I had no air left to go back the way I came or look for another way, but I couldn't get through. I thought I would pass out and drown. I forced myself to push my body upward and shoved my body through the tube of rock until I was scraped and bleeding but breaking the surface. I dragged my body to the surface.

[Note: Quoted text is excerpted from Jacob and Wilhelm Grimm's *Kinder-und Hausmärchen* (Children's and Household Tales—Grimm's Fairy Tales), no. 47, and translated by D. L. Ashliman.]

# Obituary

*Jericho Brown*

Say I never was a waiter. Say I never worked
Retail. Tell the papers and the police, I wrote

One color and wore a torn shirt. Nothing
Makes for longevity like a lie, so I had a few

Fakes and stains, but quote me, my hunger
Was sudden and wanting. I waited, marked

Time with what heart-
Beats I could hear, bumped my head nodding

At home. Some boys walked to my bedroom
In boots. Some of me woke wheezing the next

Morning wherever snow didn't fall by the foot
In a day. Beyond that, a name. For proof, a finger

Moving forward. When you measure the distance
Between this grave and what I gave, you'll find me

Here, at the end of my body and in love
With Derrick Franklin, gift of carnelian,

Lashes thick as a thumb. Some men have a mind
For marriage. Some never

Leave home. If the body is a corporation,

I was the guy in charge of blood, my man

The CEO of bone.  He kept a scandal
In my pocket.  I sucked in my gut because I wanted

The lights on.  Should a fool come looking
For money, say I was a bag boy and a nanny.

Beyond that, a nation looking backward.  A smile
That would shine like the last line of cocaine.

# On Silence

*Marc Rahe*

I can't help wanting
to not say anything
wrong on the occasion
of someone's suffering.
When I touch
a shoulder, I ask
"is this the spot?"

I can't help that, when
I looked up just when
the muted documentary
on the tube was showing
bodies on a Civil War field,
I first thought "those must
not be real bodies."

When I turned up
the volume, I learned even
the soundtrack contained silence,
as silence is contained
in the nonverbal vocalizations
of the person with cerebral palsy
indicating a need only
someone who knows her would
be confident to understand.

# ON NOCTURNAL LIGHT

*Elizabeth Robinson*

Good darkness is its own address.

Flat.  Darkness: flat

lying on top of the grooves of light.

Time's ritual, descant.  How he

fits himself inside her and where

the "good" is in its riddle, now

the rite and rung hum.  Snow

lofting up from its hillside.  Bright

roil, wail for us.  And warp this.


Rut in light.  All,


almost, toward the inside air's inflowing it puzzles


to trace.

# STARKNESS FALLS

*Drew Milne*

it will be
starkness falls
falling starkly
scorn in clover
to fretworking
the zine prose
dug duggier
the most dug
than wish rung
didn't ought to
see you shimmy
does as shimmy
is but starker

it will be
starkness falls
falling starkly
first stop mown
lawn to dishing
the dish as is
x is one that's
a real dishiness
turned tresses
the cartouche
turns achingly
beautiful say so
fall out starkness

it will be
starkness falls
falling starkly
over the drone
minded network
ooze south central
ash the clearings
star curst dudes
sew white hyphen
here and here and
stewing in trails
saying hit on that
time to the stark

it will be
starkness falls
falling starkly
the north car
park thisness
shame on each
and every went
analytical while
the grammar got
good got going
were all got off
and flamed the
night out starkly

it will be
starkness falls
falling starkly
uncouth parts
into the proofs
cue schematic
as dogma is
come again
the real lamb
can but stupor
done to larks
the pall star
shot to starkness

it will be
starkness falls
falling starkly
bird to nail
smouldering
grant screeds
to stutter still
dew plaster
calls to cusp
embrasures
in which take
the taker falls
a felt starkness

it will be
starkness falls
falling starkly
laugh to pale
hard shoulders
where should
do glacial ire
paling scene
blazers are
as who purrs
then again
simply dated
and sewn stark

it will be
starkness falls
falling starkly
one fell swoop
this is a case
of violations
the goth skip
shudderings
do nice detail
spar most of
the rest park
as the rest is
sheer starkness

# Somewhere Golden

*Hannah Gamble*

One woman said
*Clean yourself up*
*with a cocktail napkin,* so here I am
in the bathroom.
Sounds of the party.
Sounds of one man
pretending he gets the joke.
Oh, he gets the joke.
He just didn't think
it was very funny.
I can understand that man.
The bones of Tom's hands
made a fist
and told my nose
a joke, which is to say he
hit me. The resulting laughter
was quiet, but
well-sustained. People decorate
their bathrooms
like I would rather be at the beach
than in this bathroom.
I'd rather be watching swans
mate for life. Well,
not actually mating.
Okay, actually mating;
you can hardly tell
what's going on. Unlike
pornography, or unlike

a wedding ceremony. Or, no.
The wedding ceremony is more
like swans. I thought
I was just watching two people
hold hands
in front of a candle.
The people deciding
to wear flowers in the winter,
disrespectful of what the world,
bigger than us, said we could wear
or eat, like the asparagus hors d'oeuvres
insisted it was a good time
to feel like it was summer.
At the wedding I was quiet.
At the party I was quiet
until Tom found me
offensive. The homeowners
long ago had decided
I'd rather be somewhere golden
than in this bathroom.
Outside the sounds
of people making promises,
or rather, hushing a room
to condone the most public
of promises made
in front of a candle.
When I'm cleaned up
I'll find, if he was invited,
the man who played the organ,
or the priest who wears soft shoes
so he doesn't disturb the holy
spirits resting in the rafters

when he walks through
the resting cathedral,
stooping at times
to pick up flowers.

# Unharvestable Flowers

*Zach Savich*

People on this island say what

people on any island say

The sun takes

24 hours

to set

A wind-grey

fence

Reddest barbed wire

I have seen

And those flowers milk

on wheat

I couldn't get close

enough to know

if each was more than a single petal

Island horse: no

horse

stands so still or brown

# Brutal

In the park across the street

a boy rushes

from limit into limit

a kite of cardboard and

twined. I tell him the snake is air if you step on it.

I tell him the elephant's tusk extends all the way up

its face to the eye, it is an optic

nerve-tooth. And when fireflies rise like a revival tent,

bright and staked to nothing, he doesn't

call it a consolation for his verifiable powerlessness

but a further cause

# Extracts from Unkindness

*Alex Phillips*

XXIII.
It happened again that the
rainwater got so excited
coming down the street
army carrying summer
over its head on the street

XXIV.
   Make note of the insistence

and once it beats

         low
         a note

leaning on the staff

         though I tremble at the invisible

children still running
in my mind

   Seriously they don't get tired
   and the cat
   literally
   was chasing its tail

Now I am angry at the tail

whipping

around
and the surprise
when it's not there

Invite me back into the cave
where I have pictured you
so many times
and revive my vision

The ability to see
in the dark

When I look into the future
I see nothing
And when I look in the dark
I see nothing
And therefore
The future is dark
And dark is the future

When I turn out the lights
Those dreams are
what is going on
long after I am unborn again

Hopefully not like in a bad movie
or a good one even with
my arms outstretched
moaning

I know someone who would say
Yes, that sounds like you

In that halcyon light
    I mean dark
existence having no child
upon whose hopes mine are pinned

        But my clothes

Those are probably pinned on

And out comes the sun
as if it heard me and the sun is the sun is the past

    I guess

According to

                    me

But you know

They do

call me when they want
a simpler way
to see something complicated
even if it's wrong

Children out of my mind
    I regret what was done to you

I certainly do

     You know it had to be that way

I line the past with gauze

The past is like a tunnel I stare into

The edges are fuzzy
        and soft

It also means
     Go ahead and tumble
     Do your tumbling routine
        little soldiers

I haven't seen a single child
on the street outside
and I've been waiting
so I could describe
his pain his simple shield
held above his head
like the soldiers who march
with fall held high

let's all fall
     by the
     wayside
     at the high school
     and remember that
     it was the place
     where everything was

        more of a high resolution
        version

    Still
though

Gauze in the silence

The childless silence

    Instead a man with a beret
            skin tight long underwear
            sunglasses

    Oh the cats see a bird

XXVI.
when high school
calls, we puzzle it together

so what's the difference coach
            put touring feet on the pavement
            if flaws are the pavement

Work is hardly what it was
pass the bill
an inside cylindrical job

The ones where we had every tool
        we could imagine
        were the best dreams

I spent too long on
pushing the tray in line
   the metallic poor flavors
   of time

Faking in and out of a trance

From the succubus lane
   staggers in a high plains drifter
   who loves red paint so much

He got him a new hobby
       brings him out in the damndest
       weather
   britches worn like a hurricane
   he came to make a few things clear
       The first
       paint

       The second

shoot
and
it all became clear
   and the subject was forgotten

# GEOLOGIC TIME

*James Haug*

And sometimes I'm just going
Along the snow's melting where
Last I shoveled it Allison
Gives me the old thumbs up
But I somehow think she's really
Pointing at something weighing
In overhead I look up at

Nothing nothing's there I mean
A low ceiling and the invisible
Workings of major wind currents
That's all enough I say
For me now to gather and put
My shoulder into the place where
It is my shoulder should go

I'm pushing a big transparent
Stone up a steep unseen slope
Of which no one says nothing not
Even me I'm just going a-
Long hoping my neighbors regard
My gestures of good will I
Hate it too if a story intrudes

# A Good Plague

*Will Smiley*

Knocked off a good plague of its joy
Thankfully for the sake of you
It snuck the city up and left its interior.
It needed to go out of Sarah's family's home and did

To where it was carried and with it flew China's bells.
Nearest to the street it did a brother
A birthday robe and a castle is there marring his freshness.
Bring yourself unto the street for a brother's sake

And outside of your sack let yourself be wound
Knocked off a coil of a good plague
To where it shakes itself out of your homeliness
And yourself exists it because.

So it was that in the year of our Lord
Fog was preserved and the sea wasn't.

# The Snow

The snow was falling then.
Inside a zero and a season.
Everything happened in time.
An inconsistency was silently removed.

It was a dreamer and a decimal.
No use mincing words.
Nothing it said mattered.
Though it spoke in numbers
And at times even spoke well.

But who taught you anything?
I'll just lie down on the track
And wait for a train.
Roughly speaking
We will never meet again.

# The Extinct

*Keetje Kuipers*

Imagine I'm the last woman on earth,
the snowiest plover, the loneliest

deep-sea-swimming whale. It's not my fault, but
it might be. Should I keep changing until

I become something that has an other?
I've tried that. What else can I do for love?

Now not even the gray wolves listen to my
long litany of failures. They know I'm just

putting this self-sadness in my mouth—
a polar bear crunching seal bones between

her teeth—to get what little I can from it.
They still won't let me blame myself:

When I tell them my name isn't a song
to sing, they call it back to me again and again.

# The Clocks, Lobotomous

*Shara Lessley*

*FBI Crime Lab: Quantico, Virginia*

Of the three dozen or so—gold-plated,
red chrome, fish-keyed, bird-faced—
locked up like high school trophies
staged beneath display lights, it's not
the *Syracuse 8-Day* nor *German Bell*,
*Skeleton Mechanical* or *Musical Carousel*
that struck deadliest or is most eminent,
but the plainest Jane of the bunch: old
*Big Ben Westclox* ("style three"), straight-
faced with concave curves at its base,
nickel-trimmed, non-luminous. Inside
the case, time stands still: *Mickey*'s fixed
at half past three; *Dick Tracy*'s stalled
at six-o-clock (their springs have all
been clipped). Agents in badges rush
the lab: this just in—another bag from
Rudolph's ridge-top camp: cigarettes,
health food supplements, five pounds
of nails, "Suspect's Brother Cuts Off
Hand with Saw" (an *Independent* article),
King James Bible and semi-automatic
rifle, a page-frayed *Victoria's Secret*.
A team of techs sorts out the stash,
while across the lab: *Equity, New Household,*
*Ship-Bell's Victory* (all built in factories

last century) stand transfixed—holes
drilled in their foreheads through which
a current once surged bolt-to-screw
and back toward the hour at hand.
And though the exemplars' shelves
are decades thick, in this the age of
car alarms and roaming phones,
when even a doughnut
can be used to rig a bomb, change is
quick: the wind-up-clock-as-switch
is almost, if not, dead. Minutes pass
like lead. The hour grows long. "Tech
Three" labels a photo; in it, a blonde
in a tight-fitting tee holds a sign: "Run
Rudolph Run." The day's almost done.
*Big Ben* stares at the wall. At a campus
in Connecticut a pendulum swings:
the pipe's shrapnel long since set
in place; deep in the device's metal chest
a small gear rotates, drops its weight.

# Netopir noče molčati

*Miklavž Komelj*

*za Unico Zürn*

Čoln noče te poti.
Noč. Oči peče ta lina,
trn, lom pen pači nemo čelo.
In motor tone.
Očita.
Ropota. Topota. Toneč tolče.
Mir.
In čolnič noče te lepote
niča.
Mir.
Miiirr.
Netopir: Nočem
molčati.

# THE BAT WON'T SHUT ITS TRAP

*for Unica Zürn*

The boat don't like that tack.
The night. That porthole hurts the eyes,
a thorn, the foam breaks, makes faces on a silent forehead.
And a motor sinks.
Whines.
Rattles. Clatters. Sinks and cracks.
Peace.
And the baby boat don't want that trifling
beauty.
Peace.
Peeeace.
The bat: I won't shut
my trap.

\*\*\*

ptiči med sončnim mrkom—
*njihova* nenadna
                    tišina,
natančna do delca sekunde—
se je sprožil avtomatizem?—
ali skrajno pozorno sledenje
procesu?—kjer drhti svet—
brez nadaljevanja
                    sveta


. . .

z brnečimi srci

\*\*\*

birds during a solar eclipse—
*their* sudden
                    silence,
exact to a fraction of a second—
did the machinery spring open?—
or was it the extremely attentive next step
in a process?—where a world trembled—
without continuing
                    itself


. . .
with droning hearts


*Translated from the Slovenian by Dan Rosenberg and Boris Gregoric.*

# This is a Test of the Internal Emergency Broadcast System

*Lisa Olstein*

On her way home from school
your little girl wants spotted mice
from the pet store.

She wants to give them a bath
without losing them in the suds
but they escape their paper bag

and disappear underfoot in the car.
Now your little girl wants
a bright green snake

that won't get lost in the snow.
The red-tipped posts lining
the drive look wounded.

This is not an emergency.
This is winter saying I decapitated
your small glass bird.

Hungry deer step from the woods
on velvet-gloved legs.
This is a test.

Place your elevated heart
rate in this pre-paid self-addressed

steel envelope.

We should all be prepared
to proceed calmly
through the crackling air.

# Teaching Farm

They put a plug in the cow
to stop the hole they carved in its flank
for recruits to plunge their arms into
feeling for spoons and pasture debris.
Mulch accomplishes what?
Insulates the brains of dormant tubers.
Moss accomplishes what?
Salves the edges of jagged stones
the dog will not fetch.
The dog is fierce out of fear,
the instructor says holding a cloth
to the deliveryman's bleeding leg.
Everyone's crying from the pepper
spray that misfired in the wind.
They all carry it now plus biscuits.
We stand around on a field of fiery green
squares thick with researched seed.
The field looks like a pinwheel
to the balloonist floating the near sky.
It's his first time and he thought it'd be more
peaceful but the gas keeps firing
and he can't control the drift of his glide.
It's like the air is arguing all around him
and he really doesn't care what we have for dinner
as long as we can sit down and eat.

# DOOR OUT. OUT

*Eryn Green*

Feeling on the mend
Moving toward Shangri-La
I guess. I'll keep you
posted
—
Dear Cold,
Out. Out
I wake to the sound
of cars in my chest
Out. My throat, out. My nose
Out so that nothing that is not
Green can go out. Green out
and Green in—the trees outside my friend Kathryn
has said so many perfect things
I hardly know where to begin
some about her nose
some about heaven
The milky way paints a giant S in the sky

# DESIGNATED DRIVER

*Daniela Olszewska*

you are trying out
all four versions
of yr indoor voice,
but the passengers
are demanding
an AM station,
a rather ruthless joke,
+ an explanation
for all these candy
bar wrappers.
when the speed
limit ups to 55,
you start remembering
about elvis
+ the way the gas
station attendant
kept asking
if the hetero half
of yr heart
had even a little
bit of tennessee
left in it.

# I AM RUNNING OUT OF QUANTITY;
# I AM RUNNING OUT OF QUALITY

so, fine, there's a stable
full of red seahorses

tethered
to my side of the bed

+ i'm merging back
into that half-blazed

feeling again. after the scalpoff,
most of the furniture

is really starting to look
like it belongs

in a school of dentistry.
i'm trying to get them

to leave me siren-made
+ in the corner. it can't possibly

be time for another hour
of smelling salt therapies.

this morning, when i woke
up w/welters on my operagoing

bone, i realized that i really

need to start getting used

to making do with my third
+ fourth best options.

# Sonsmanship

*Sean Bishop*

I woke and was an animal. The first branch
swung by a chimp, which made him king, hung
about where you'd expect it to. I decided then
I would never again call my mother; I'd gulp down
the first frail nest of eggs I found. Oh Mom,
there is this cruel appendage between us, there is
a thicket of hair as tough as the brush
our great great ape-daddy rose above.
Right this moment you are probably quilting
or combing the hair of your barely-a-dog
who has pissed on everything in the house to claim it,
to show his love. Soon the season of gifts
and potatoes will be upon us. Soon you will make,
for everyone, a kind of new womb in which
to wrap themselves—even after the dog
has burned in the vet's red kiln, even after
I have lifted you into the rough-shod box
I've already begun, swinging the hammer
as if it were the only part of myself
I knew how to use in shame.

# Position in Time

*Lisa Fishman*

The cat's face  /  the fox's face  /  6 rides 5 dollars in June

Arrange the furniture around the trees
in a confusion of time and face

The willowleaves turn the brightest green
not red or yellow
if that's a willow
outside your window
If it's October again

the size of acorns

To ride in the serpent or microscope, unbutton your shoes

please

The cat and the fox were one
illusion out the second-story window, straight across
into another second-story window, out of which the animal uncanny
    stared back

How carefully it floats

# In Stead a Form

That the plant may leaf
out into leafing—perhaps—imprinted I heard
this pattern before
JUST LOOK

How many birds
in the eaves of a roof / If all the avenues in Avignon
were bridged by bridges then the song
would lengthen also

could be the sun
striking the ear—JUST SO

The blank rabbit in the green field is a half-
rabbi   half the shoe
was stuffed with grass

why anyone are flown


            ::


The body be golden okay
plant onions to flower or wild grow
silent in face of it: fact
upon fact

What the yellow swallowtail eats has the wrong name:
prickly ash, neither prickly

nor ash, yet try
to posit as turning

the river the swimmer can
daylight, can current, can merge
in stead a form

Later the jewelweed goes in a bowl, turns upon contact
into its name—gleams—do not describe
How change it some

is synonym for love
How if it
served for chair for table & for bed
repair the ocean & the swath

# Hi, Again

*Jordan Stempleman*

It looks like I've done something terrible,
unforgivable, but all I've done is butchered
a pomegranate while listening to cartoons.
Who really gives a shit about fruit and its
triumphant preciousness, its leaking, its
lies about what I am and what I have done?
The older plant, on the dreary days, goes,
racism is an anthology, this water my fists,
no other, nothing more numerous or spread
from twig to twig. Child, you should take
yourself out for a glass of water, feel what
it's like to go where each cluster of bursting
fruit is nothing but hearing too much about
what I have done. Like, I'm ringing the neck
of another little, blind fish. He shudders
so much harder than what's going on now.
And when I rehearse, maybe in the house,
maybe with a package under my arm, but
with my forehead I sigh, and with my skies
I edge towards a moment that keeps all
I notice in front of me, the protest I'm afraid
of will be of a time when choice was the same
as enough, various the occasion to forgive me.

# Muscle Mystery Sutra

*Ben Kopel*

This is where / all of my ideas / they come from / a humming / in the air ducts / here is something / I owe all of you / all will be well / the thrill-ride buzz / of cartoon sand / kicked in faces / is faster / than your excuses / this is someone saying / we had to break your heart / to get to the miracle / between the muscles / there is a place / there is nothing there / for you / jacked apart / I am / unsleeping / barefoot / on the beach / my brain is a star / and alone / I am strong / and we / we grow weaker / like a swimmer / but no one / will be humiliated / this time I am playing my tune / in tune / and I play said song / I repeat / on repeat / so much so / eventually I believe / that the tune / I'm into / is all that I am / to be / maybe / finally / enough

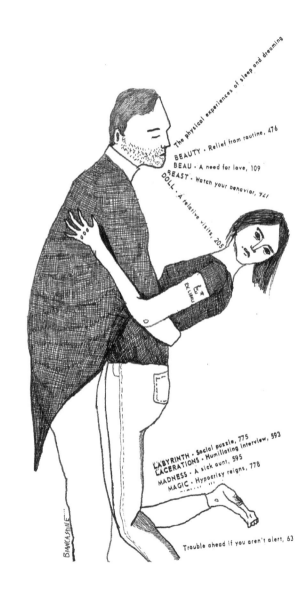

# I'm Aware of the Animals Within Me

*S. E. Smith*

My world is such a beautiful place:

Jacqueline Susann wrote a whole book about her dog,
most people are made of water and fat,
most candy is either chocolatey or fruity,

but there's something to be said
for choco-fruity combo.

True, there are some jobs that you grow out of
like ballerina, but there are always others, like dog-catcher,
that you get better at with age.

There are varieties of toothpick for show
and function both, and in the hallway
of the karaoke parlor you can hear
every song that exists sung with enthusiasm.

You can add your mystery to the others
piled with the coats on the bed at the party.
You can tell a joke about babies because
the babies all around will not take offense.

Nietzsche said: altruism is nothing
but the selfish desires of others

which might mean altruism is nothing
but the selfish desires of Nietzsche

but it's also possible I'm so hopeful
that it makes me a little dumb about Germans.

It is a beautiful world where you can be dumb about Germans.

You can sleep with fire and not get burned
if you convince your boyfriend that he is a fire

and when he burns you anyway, always some
fireman will show up just in time.

It ended the day he drove you around
Santa Barbara, lost for two hours while your fever spiked—
the chimes of his missed jokes refracting against each other

until they became a solid, tangible thing, like a log,
eventually two logs, multiple logs that at some point
yielded to an organizing principle and became

the cabin in which you now live, alone.
It is shabby but nice; in this it resembles you.

Vinho verde goes great with the fish.

Lenny Bruce died of sadness.

People will always laugh if your hair is messed up
and you say, "I'm going for that wind-blown look"

because you look great that way, you really do.

Because after all this music, there is the music
of what comes after, like a hole left in the air

after you've thrown your body through it.

::

Of course the complaints are valid:
not enough water in the well, and what's there
smells like an offending ham,

so much snow that the trees look a lot
like chubby Russian folk dolls,

and boiled cabbage will trail you for days
until you trick it with cigarette smoke
or pork chops or a marathon of procedural cop dramas.
Exploring the harmonics of an empty
beer can, I arrived at a theory

of melodic counterpoint, which,
big surprise, involves emptiness
refracting against itself until it becomes
a solid, tangible thing which yields
eventually to an organizing principal
and becomes the song I now sing, alone.

Seneca said: quit fucking around
and don't go into politics.

Nobody knows how we decide what we love.
Seneca sure didn't know. A tin roof
tunes the sunlight, tree pollen
falling like dirty snow.

::

In spite of those certainties I find it encouraging,
how bored rural teenagers can imitate any hairdo
with hair spray and scotch tape

and how adults have a shitty time at the zoo
but will take the kids there anyway.

Dancing to the radio can alleviate the ache
of the mind, but only if you dance
like you are a bad, bad man.

Schiller said: discretion is the better part
of aesthetics. Believe it.

Similarly, the nature of gym memberships is deceit
but it turns out that the deceived look
extremely attractive, full of life.

I like to think about animals doing people things
because a lot of the things I want to do
to other people are inhumane and ridiculous

but when you imagine bears doing their taxes,
spreading out the shoebox of receipts
on a green plaid couch and vowing

to save up for a newer, safer sedan

it seems like we have a lot in common
and could peacably share a dinner of salmon bellies.

Vinho verde goes great with the fish.

Sad people are too enthusiastic about cookies.

This is how you will be able to tell them apart
from the others, whose hungers are more general.

::

Overnight, the night insects came back,
mosquitoes carrying small parts of me away
so they can put me back together later
in a new all-blood format.

I will be pure and total and spared
the chore of dressing for my funeral.

There is no way to spare yourself
from dressing for your mother's funeral
unless you die first. There it is,
the awful thing I sing in spite of.

There it is, the mosquito whining
in each room after the light goes out,
tuning the house's emptiness
like the ringing in my mother's ears
which she is told will not stop

so it's not really a song,
just something to get used to.

Flaubert said: it's okay if your life is boring.

Seneca said: life is long if you know
how to use it.

I say the air tonight is as warm as a bath
and whatever you think of the one
who drew it for you, whatever
creation myth you subscribe to,
and whether you feel mostly
like a head poked through a plywood
cut-out at the fair, a tiny head
riding the shoulders of a giant

doesn't matter. You are here,
you are its celebrant.

::

I'm going for that wind-blown look.

I'm making a pompadour out of hair spray
and scotch tape, a cape for containing
the gesture of where I am coming from.

I am coming from the middle of things,
swimming pools where my uncles
keep their socks on to hide their white
ankles, bright as halogens.

It's not really a song unless
it yields to an organizing principle

the way my mother convinces herself
that the ringing in her ears is actually
the spring frogs back early
in spite of three feet of snow

and makes a song out of the blood
rushing in her head.

::

Just as chickweed chokes out the ivy
and the sun turns its back on the statue,

just as the houses turn blue in the cold
and windows orange as it gets darker,

just as the snow melts on the ridge tops
but stays behind, insolent in the nettle pit,

I am coming ever closer to you.
I am watching from not far away.

Just as buds crust the dogwood's branches
and wasps set out their black longboats,

just as the bathtub begins to stink like mud
and gloves are forgotten in coat pockets

and bad habits are forgiven, and even the furnace
is forgiven for muttering all day long

I am getting closer to you, I am always
ever closer.

# Contributors

LJUBICA ARSOVSKA has worked on English translations of plays, poems, short stories, and novels, including Dimkovska's *Do Not Awaken Them with Hammers*. She is editor-in-chief of *Kulturen zivot*, the leading cultural magazine in Macedonia.

JOHN ASHBERY's most recent collection of poems is *Planisphere*. His *Collected Poems 1956–1987* was published in 2008, and his translation of Arthur Rimbaud's *Illuminations* was published in 2011. He is the 2011 recipient of the National Book Foundation's Medal for Distinguished Contribution to American Letters and was recently honored with a National Humanities Medal at the White House.

SEAN BISHOP teaches in the MFA Program at UW-Madison. He is the former managing editor of *Gulf Coast* and the founding editor of *Better* (bettermagazine.org). His poems appear in *Alaska Quarterly Review, Boston Review, Crazyhorse, Indiana Review, Ploughshares, Poetry*, and elsewhere.

JERICHO BROWN is recipient of the Whiting Writers award and a fellowship from the Radcliffe Institute at Harvard University. His poems appear in *The American Poetry Review* and *The Believer*. His first book, *PLEASE*, won the American Book Award.

MACGREGOR CARD is the author of a poetry collection, *Duties of an English Foreign Secretary*, and a chapbook, *The Archers*. He serves as associate editor at the Modern Language Association and teaches poetry at Pratt Institute.

FRANCESCA CHABRIER lives and writes in Massachusetts. Her poems can be found in places like *notnostrums, Sixth Finch, Action Yes*, and more. Her chapbook, *The Axioms*, is forthcoming from Pilot Books.

LIDIJA DIMKOVSKA was born in 1971 in Skopje, Macedonia. She attained a doctoral degree in Romanian poetry in Bucharest. She lives in Ljubljana, Slovenia, teaching World Literature in Nova Gorica and translating Slovenian and Romanian literature in Macedonian.

JOSHUA EDWARDS directs and coedits Canarium Books. He's the author of *Campeche* (with photographs by his father, Van Edwards) and *Imperial Nostalgias* (forthcoming), and the translator of Mexican poet María Baranda's *Ficticia*.

JOE FLETCHER's work can be found in *Octopus, Slope, Painted Bride Quarterly, Puerto Del Sol, Hollins Critic*, and elsewhere. He lives in Carrboro, North Carolina.

LISA FISHMAN's most recent books are *Flowercart* and *Current*. She lives in Orfordville, Wisconsin, and teaches at Columbia College Chicago.

LEWIS FREEDMAN lives in Madison and coruns the _____-Shaped reading series with Andy Gricevich, with whom he also edits and publishes chapbooks for *cannot exist*. Lewis coedits the publication of chapbooks with Agnes Fox Press. Three chapbooks have been published under his name: *The Third Word*, *Catfish Po' Boys*, and *SUFFERING EXCHANGE WALKS WITH AND*.

HANNAH GAMBLE is the author of *Your Invitation to a Modest Breakfast*, selected by Bernadette Mayer for the 2011 National Poetry Series and to be published by Fence in 2012. Her poems and interviews appear or are forthcoming in *APR*, *The Laurel Review*, *Indiana Review*, *Ecotone*, and elsewhere.

ERYN GREEN is a doctoral candidate at the University of Denver. Recently his collection, *Eruv*, was selcted by C. D. Wright as a finalist for the 2011 Omnidawn 1st/2nd Book Prize. Eryn's work has appeared or is forthcoming in *Colorado Review*, *the tiny*, *Bat City Review*, *H_NGM_N*, and *Word for/ Word*, among others.

BORIS GREGORIC is a Croatian-American short story writer, visual artist, translator, and language tutor. The author of five books of short fiction, he has translated prose and poetry between English, Croatian, and Slovene.

JAMES HAUG's most recent collections include *Legend of the Recent Past* and two chapbooks, *Why I Like Chapbooks* and *Scratch*.

MARY HICKMAN is a graduate of the Iowa Writers' Workshop. She lives in Iowa City where she runs Cosa Nostra Editions with Robert Fernandez and makes artists' books with the Center for the Book.

EMILY HUNT's poems have appeared or are forthcoming in *Conduit*, *Sixth Finch*, *Sea Ranch*, and *SoftSpot*. Find her at ehunt.tumblr.com.

ELAINE KAHN is the author of the chapbook *Customer*. She is the assistant editor of Flowers & Cream Press and cocurates the LOOT performance series at Flying Object. Elaine performs music under the name Horsebladder.

MIKLAVŽ KOMELJ is a Slovenian poet, essayist, and art historian. He has published six books of poetry, a collection of essays, and a study of the art of the Yugoslav partisans in World War II. He has also published Slovene translations of works by Fernando Pessoa, Pier Paolo Pasolini, and César Vallejo.

BEN KOPEL lives in New Orleans, Louisiana. He is the author of a chapbook, *Because We Must*, and a full-length collection, *VICTORY*. "Muscle Mystery Sutra" is for Susanna McBride.

KEETJE KUIPERS was the Margery Davis Boyden Wilderness Writing Resident and a Wallace Stegner Fellow. Her book, *Beautiful in the Mouth*, won the A. Poulin, Jr. Poetry Prize from BOA Editions. She is the Emerging Writer Lecturer at Gettysburg College.

NICK LANTZ is the author of the poetry collections *We Don't Know We Don't Know*, *The Lightning that Strikes the Neighbors' House*, and *How to Dance When You Do Not Know How to Dance* (forthcoming). Work from this issue is part of a series of lyric plays in his current poetry manuscript-in-progress, *you, beast*.

DOROTHEA LASKY is the author of *AWE*, *Black Life*, and the forthcoming *Thunderbird*, all from Wave Books. She is also the author of several chapbooks, including *Poetry Is Not a Project*. She has taught at New York University and Wesleyan University. She currently lives in New York City and can be found online at www.birdinsnow.com.

PAUL LEGAULT is the cofounder of the translation press Telephone Books and the author of three books of poetry: *The Madeleine Poems*, *The Other Poems*, and *The Emily Dickinson Reader*.

SHARA LESSLEY's poems have appeared in *Ploughshares*, *Kenyon Review*, *Southern Review*, *Cincinnati Review*, and *The Nation*, among others. Her collection, *Two-Headed Nightingale*, is forthcoming. She currently lives in Amman, Jordan.

NATALIE LYALIN is the author of *Pink and Hot Pink Habitat* and the chapbook *Try A Little Time Travel*. She lives in Philadelphia.

SHANE MCCRAE is the author of *Mule* and two chapbooks, *One Neither One* and *In Canaan*. His work has appeared, or is forthcoming, in *The Best American Poetry 2010*, *The American Poetry Review*, *Fence*, *Agni*, *Denver Quarterly* and others. He lives in Iowa City.

DREW MILNE is the Judith E. Wilson Lecturer in Drama & Poetry at the University of Cambridge. His books include *Go Figure*, *Mars Disarmed*, *The Damage: new and selected poems*, and *Bench Marks*. Visit his website at drewmilne.tripod.com.

LISA OLSTEIN is the author of *Radio Crackling, Radio Gone* and *Lost Alphabet*. A new collection, *Little Stranger*, is forthcoming in 2013. She is the lyricist for the band Cold Satellite fronted by singer-songwriter Jeffrey Foucault.

DANIELA OLSZEWSKA is the author of three forthcoming collections of poetry: *cloudfang : : cakedirt*, *Citizen J*, and *How To Feel Comfortable With*

*Your Special Talents* (cowritten with Carol Guess).

KIKI PETROSINO is the author of *Fort Red Border* and the coeditor of *Transom* (transomjournal.com). She teaches literature and creative writing at the University of Louisville. Her latest collection of poems is forthcoming in 2013.

ALEX PHILLIPS is director of Assessment and Curriculum Development at Commonwealth Honors College. His work has appeared in places such as *Poetry, Open City, notnostrums,* and *American Life in Poetry.* His book, *Crash Dome,* is published by Factory Hollow Press.

MARC RAHE is the author of *The Smaller Half.* His poems have appeared or are forthcoming in *GutCult, Mrs. Maybe, Mudfish, notnostrums,* and *Sixth Finch,* among others.

PEGGY REID is a translator of Macedonian poetry and prose. She has received many awards, including the Macedonian Literary Translators' Society Award and two first prizes at the Stratford-upon-Avon Poetry Festival for her own poetry. She teaches English at the Saints Cyril and Methodius University.

ELIZABETH ROBINSON is the author of *Three Novels* and the forthcoming *Counterpart.* With Colleen Lookingbill, she recently edited *As if it Fell from the Sun,* an anthology of women's

poetry. A recent recipient of a grant from the Boomerang Foundation, Robinson is currently the Hugo Fellow at the University of Montana.

LEE ANN RORIPAUGH is the author of *On the Cusp of a Dangerous Year, Year of the Snake,* and *Beyond Heart Mountain.* She's the director of Creative Writing at the University of South Dakota, and editor-in-chief of *South Dakota Review.*

DAN ROSENBERG's *The Crushing Organ* won the 2011 American Poetry Journal Book Prize; it will be published in 2012. His poems, translations, and book reviews have appeared recently in *American Letters & Commentary, Kenyon Review Online,* and *Gulf Coast.*

TOMAŽ ŠALAMUN lives in Ljubljana, Slovenia. He taught spring semester 2011 at Michener Center for Writers at the University of Texas. His recent books translated into English are *Woods and Chalices, Poker, There's the Hand and There's the Arid Chair,* and *The Blue Tower.*

ZACH SAVICH teaches at Shippensburg University. He is the author of four books, including *Events Film Cannot Withstand* and *The Firestorm.* His newest collection of poetry, *Century-Swept Brutal,* is forthcoming.

LAUREN SHAPIRO is the author of the chapbook *Yo-Yo Logic* and the poetry collection *Easy Math,* forthcoming in 2013. She lives in Madison, Wisconsin.

WILL SMILEY lives in Iowa City.

S. E. SMITH is the author of *I Live in a Hut*, winner of the 2011 CSU Poetry Center's first book prize. She is a graduate of the Michener Center for Writers and Carnegie Mellon University; her work has appeared in *Fence*, *Best New Poets*, *Black Warrior Review*, and others; and she is the founding editor of *OH NO* magazine.

JORDAN STEMPLEMAN's most recent collections of poetry are *No, Not Today* and *Doubled Over*. He coedits *The Continental Review*, teaches writing and literature at the Kansas City Institute, and curates A Common Sense Reading Series.

BIANCA STONE is a poet and artist. She is the author of *I Want To Open The Mouth God Gave You Beautiful Mutant*. Her newest book is a collaboration with Anne Carson, *Antigonick*, an illustrated translation of *Antigone*.

MICHAEL THOMAS TAREN's translations of Tomaž Šalamun's work appear in the anthologies *7 Poets, 4 Days, 1 Book* and *Slovene Sampler*, as well as in journals such as *Chicago Review*, *A Public Space*, *Poetry Review*, *Fulcrum*, *Colorado Review*, and *Circumference*. He is a graduate of the Iowa Writer's Workshop.

JONO TOSCH lives in Massachusetts. He teaches fermentation workshops in church rec rooms and creative laboratories. You can find his antifood blog food blog at oilchanges.blogspot.com.

# praise for POSt roaD